"Steeped in the legal profession, adept argument, the author clearly takes with sober seriousness truth, the rules of logic, and the dictates of fair play. This happy conjunction enables the book to showcase a powerful legal mind applying his trade and prodigious gifts to questions of enduring importance and matters that matter. The book provides a valuable apologetic contribution to our fraught cultural moment. Lanier's consistent commitment to clear definition, reasonable inference, and uncommon common sense serve as a refreshing corrective to the poor inferential habits, selective evidence, and confirmation bias ubiquitous today. Enthusiastically recommended."

David Baggett, professor of philosophy and director of the Center for the Foundations of Ethics at Houston Baptist University

"For too long Christian belief has been subjected to uncritical scrutiny. Finally Mark Lanier, a lawyer of the first order, places disbelief before the bar. This book is a fair and balanced legal proceeding against the point of view that denies the existence of God and the redemptive results of faith on our culture."

Michael Card, writer, songwriter

"When trial lawyer Mark Lanier steps into the courtroom, the case for atheism dissolves. Like a well-prepared, determined prosecutor, Lanier goes on the attack and leaves the atheist defenseless. The reader will sit in the jury box and find atheism guilty. Even more, Lanier makes a case for faith. This book is compelling."

Jerry Root, professor emeritus, Wheaton College

"This book effectively lays out the wide-ranging, relevant evidence for the biblical God while exposing atheism's consistent failure to explain the way things are in the world. Of particular interest is that a seasoned, highly acclaimed lawyer takes the reader through it step by step, drawing on his own experience and illustrating how rules of evidence work. The book is an engaging, fascinating, and illuminating read."

Paul Copan, Pledger Family Chair of Philosophy and Ethics at Palm Beach Atlantic University and author of *Loving Wisdom: A Guide to Philosophy and Christian Faith*

"A leading trial lawyer assesses the role of evidence in atheism, agnosticism, and Christianity. This is a witty, very engaging, and original contribution to one of the great debates of our age. Highly recommended."

Alister McGrath, professor of science and religion at Oxford University

"In *Atheism on Trial*, Mark Lanier has produced a clear, concise, and worthy companion to *Christianity on Trial*. With the sensibilities and skills that come with being one of the most successful trial lawyers in US history, Lanier carefully dissects and deconstructs the arguments posed by advocates of atheism and its more congenial sister, agnosticism. After closing arguments, the underpinnings of atheistic philosophy are found wanting, and a case for the Christian faith prevails."

David B. Capes, senior research professor at the Lanier Theological Library

W. MARK LANIER

ATHEISM

ON TRIAL

A LAWYER EXAMINES THE

CASE FOR UNBELIEF

An imprint of InterVarsity Press
Downers Grove, Illinois

Davis, Franks, Sach — see if this makes sense.

Mark Lanier

InterVarsity Press
P.O. Box 1400, Downers Grove, IL 60515-1426
ivpress.com
email@ivpress.com

InterVarsity Press® is the book-publishing division of InterVarsity Christian Fellowship/USA®, a movement of students and faculty active on campus at hundreds of universities, colleges, and schools of nursing in the United States of America, and a member movement of the International Fellowship of Evangelical Students. For information about local and regional activities, visit intervarsity.org.

Scripture quotations, unless otherwise noted, are from The Holy Bible, English Standard Version, copyright © 2001 by Crossway Bibles, a division of Good News Publishers. Used by permission. All rights reserved.

While any stories in this book are true, some names and identifying information may have been changed to protect the privacy of individuals.

The publisher cannot verify the accuracy or functionality of website URLs used in this book beyond the date of publication.

Figure 3.1. Maarten van Heemskerck, Justitia (Justice), Städel Museum / Wikimedia Commons
Figure 10.1. "The God Seb supporting Nut on Heaven," in E. A. Wallis Budge, The Gods of the Egyptians, vol. II (Chicago: The Open Court Publishing Co., 1904) / Wikimedia Commons, Oksmith
Figure 10.2. Relief image on the Tablet of Shamash, British Library / Wikimedia Commons, Prioryman
Figure 10.3. Biblical view of the cosmos figure by InterVarsity Press

Cover design and image composite: David Fassett
Interior design: Jeanna Wiggins
Image: gavel: © CHIARI_VFX / iStock / Getty Images

ISBN 978-1-5140-0226-1 (print)
ISBN 978-1-5140-0227-8 (digital)

Printed in the United States of America ♾

InterVarsity Press is committed to ecological stewardship and to the conservation of natural resources in all our operations. This book was printed using sustainably sourced paper.

Library of Congress Cataloging-in-Publication Data
A catalog record for this book is available from the Library of Congress.

P	25	24	23	22	21	20	19	18	17	16	15	14	13	12	11	10	9	8	7	6	5	4	3	2	1
Y	39	38	37	36	35	34	33	32	31	30	29	28	27	26	25	24	23	22							

I dedicate this book to my wonderful Becky,

with love and devotion.

CONTENTS

A LEGAL PRIMER

I LIVE WITH ONE FOOT in the world of law and one in the world of faith. For almost forty years, I have earned my living working in courtrooms across America and throughout the Western world. The life blood of a just court is truth. Courts exist to ferret out the truths that matter most in life. In courtrooms, society resolves disputes peaceably rather than by force. Judges and juries make decisions whether people should forfeit their property, their freedoms, or even their lives. Courts determine which divorcing parent is, in truth, fitter to rear a child. When operating at their best, courts are civilization's best tool for getting to the core truth about life's greatest issues.

My other foot is in the world of faith. As a disclaimer, and by way of introduction, the reader should know that I am a religious person. I believe there is a God and that he has revealed himself to humanity. I am a Christian by faith. Prior to law school, I took a degree in biblical languages (Hebrew and Greek) and have worked with the Bible over forty years.

Both of those feet—the one walking in law and the one walking in faith—belong to me. I move freely between those two worlds, and often I find the worlds merge. This book is a fruit of such a merger. As a lawyer, my legal training, both in law school and on the job, has affected the way I think, research, evaluate options, and make decisions.

It intersects with my faith in what I believe and why I believe it. I am first and foremost a man of evidence. My life's work is built on evidence and arguments. Without it, my law firm doors would close. So in my faith walk, I analyze evidence and arguments. It is the way I think.

Law school begins with an orientation. For most of one week, the professors give a warm-up to the incoming class, explaining the basics of what lies ahead. Forty years ago, I was one of those students listening to a professor explain that law school would change us.

"It changes the way you think," he explained. He continued, "You won't notice it at first, but there will be signs. One morning over breakfast you will find yourself reading the warranty on the toaster—and enjoying it!"

Law school drives critical thinking and precision of thought. Generally, most students already have a bent toward that direction. The Law School Admission Test (LSAT) that every law school applicant takes is basically a logic test. If you can't score well on the logic test, you don't get into law school, much less graduate and pass the bar exam.

Law students take a range of different legal courses, each instructing the lawyers-to-be how to research carefully, think logically, and identify errors in thought. Sometimes the teaching does so directly (one of our courses was called Research and Writing); other times the new skill set underlies the legal rulings or rules of law you learn. For example, a law school evidence class is typically based on the Federal Rules of Evidence. You learn what is hearsay, and why it is generally excluded from evidence. You also learn what hearsay is admissible, the exceptions to the hearsay rule that are deemed credible enough for consideration. Those rules are the culmination of Western thought on how to discern relevant, careful evidence suitable for proving guilt or innocence with enough confidence to take someone's life, liberty, or property.

The Rules of Evidence are based on logic. The rules include logical determinations of whether evidence is relevant or irrelevant to an argument. There are rules that inspect and ensure the authenticity of evidence. In addition to the actual rules, students read and learn cases where courts have interpreted those rules. These case decisions become additional laws that guide other courts. For example, the Supreme Court set up guidelines for when opinion testimony meets the necessary academic and logical rigors to validate its usage.[1]

In a trial, lawyers use those rules to present disputes to juries and other tribunals for "findings of fact." Successful trial lawyers must be adept at identifying arguments that do not meet the necessary logical rigors for consideration. This is what frequently makes the television and movies as a lawyer stands up saying something like, "Objection, your honor; assumes facts not in evidence!"

EVIDENCE—TYPES

In this book, I will discuss the evidence for and against certain beliefs. A lot of non-lawyers speak of evidence but have a very limited view of it. Evidence in the legal arena is all-encompassing. For example, courts use scientific evidence, which is critical in assessing claims about the material world of science. But scientific evidence is limited in what it can prove. For example, it can never be used to prove a motive or the knowledge of an individual. Yet motive and knowledge clearly exist and, in certain cases, must be proven by evidence. So courts use evidence of all types, not simply scientific evidence. The key is that the evidence must be credible in the field from which it is offered.

These rules of evidence, and the legal system built around these rules, provide the best tools civilization has developed to answer difficult questions about matters past, present, and future. Courts determine things as diverse as whether someone ran a red light, whether spouses love each other, and whether one is likely to need surgical intervention years down the road.

Sometimes there is direct evidence for the matters being proven. By this courts mean there is an eyewitness who can testify to the matter based on personal knowledge. This is the person who says, "Donny

Driver ran the red light. I know this because I saw him driving a car through the light at a time where I could also see his light was red."

Often scientific evidence is direct evidence. If I want to prove benzene is in drinking water, there is a conclusive test for that. However, even scientific evidence is frequently open to interpretation.

Most of the time, however, cases don't have much direct testimony. Most times the key evidence is circumstantial. That means the circumstances lead to the conclusion. The classic law school example distinguishing between direct and circumstantial evidence is proving whether it is raining outside. Going out and personally experiencing the rain is direct evidence. Staying inside but hearing thunder and the patter of water on the windowpanes, and seeing people come in with wet umbrellas and clothes is circumstantial evidence.

In a case like Donny Driver and Plaintiff Peggy, I might need to prove how much Peggy suffered from the collision before dying. Without Peggy to give direct testimony, I would need to rely on circumstantial testimony. I would offer evidence of how long she was conscious after the wreck, what her body was going through because of the injuries, and so on.

Circumstantial evidence is just as reliable as direct evidence. Often it is the only type of evidence available. It makes sense that it can be as valuable if one considers the classic illustration of a murder case. If a murder is committed where there is an actual eyewitness, that witness can testify, and the defendant be convicted. The testimony of the eyewitness would be considered direct testimony. The testimony directly addresses whether a defendant is guilty.

But circumstantial testimony can also serve to convict a murderer, and this is important because very few murders have eyewitnesses. Circumstantial testimony includes things like discovery of a murder weapon, finding fingerprints of the defendant on the murder weapon, motive, opportunity, invalid alibis, and the like. Judges routinely instruct juries that they are to consider circumstantial evidence.

I have tried many fraud cases. In fraud cases, I must prove that the defendant intentionally deceived another. I have yet to see a fraud case where there is direct evidence of the "intent" element of fraud. Intent is a personal, subjective thought process. There are no eyewitnesses to intent other than the one who is deceiving. No one comes right out and says, "Yes, I misled Mr. So and So on purpose! I wanted him to rely on my misrepresentation to his own detriment!" I prove intent through circumstantial evidence: motive, knowledge, opportunity, and so on.

EVIDENCE—CREDIBILITY

Courts also recognize that some evidence is more credible than other evidence. This might be because of the kind of evidence. For example, I was trying a case over whether the drug Vioxx could cause a myocardial infarction (a heart attack). Some studies were double-blinded randomized trials involving thousands of patients. Those studies were more credible than a case report of how the drug worked in a single individual.

Credibility involves many factors, including the reliability of a witness. Credibility is very important. It determines how authoritative the evidence is deemed to be.

I recently tried a case over whether a type of artificial hip implant was defective. The implant was made of a metal ball rubbing against a metal cup. I believed that the metal debris from the rubbing had destroyed the tissue in my plaintiffs' hips (there were five plaintiffs in this trial). I put on my case, setting out the evidence from tissue samples, from documents, and from an array of experts, including one of the world's preeminent orthopedic surgeons who said he never used metal-on-metal hip implants because of concerns over their safety. After I concluded my case, the defendant manufacturer's lawyers began putting on the company's case. One of their witnesses was an orthopedic surgeon who swore that metal-on-metal hip implants were fine.

The witness made a good impression at first, but then I started to cross-examine him. I began my cross-examination by pointing out that the witness had received royalties from implant manufacturers. In other words, he was getting paid by the companies that made products like the one at issue in the case. This was relevant on whether he had an unbiased opinion. The actual transcript of the trial reads,

> **Q.** (by me) "You're one of these royalty type people. You've been paid by my count $6,870,362.69 in royalties, haven't you?"
>
> **A.** "I actually don't accept that number. I don't think it's even been close to that."

I then began to detail what he was paid. I listed one type of implant called a Mallory-Head system where I asserted he'd been paid $1.4 million dollars for that implant alone. The transcript recorded his response,

> **A.** "I think you're getting me mixed up with somebody else. I've never had royalty in the Mallory-Head system . . . I think you're just making things up. I'll try to keep you on the straight and narrow, but already you have said things that are untrue."

At this point credibility was in play, both his and mine. If I could prove he had received those royalties, the jury would know he either had a very poor memory, or he was dishonest in his testimony. Either way, his credibility would be shot.

The judge rested us for the day, and we started again the next morning. I went straight back to the credibility issue. The record from the next morning reads,

> **Q.** "Sir, one of the things you said yesterday that I found disturbing— it's on page 248 of the record starting at line 12. You said to me: 'I think you're just making things up.' And you said it with earnestness in your voice. Do you remember that testimony?"
>
> **A.** "Yes, I do."

I then began showing check after check labeled "royalty payment" made out to the doctor, mailed to his home address, for the Mallory-Head system, and showing that for years he regularly received royalty payments and that they added up well in excess of the amount I had asserted.

The jury had heard this doctor's evidence, but now his credibility was next to nothing. He wasn't honest, and it was evident. That called into question the entirety of his testimony. Now just because someone is dishonest, it doesn't mean that everything they say is wrong. But it increases caution and suspicion about what they say, especially if it is solely opinion testimony.

So as I weigh evidence, and as a jury weighs evidence in the legal system in a trial, nothing is taken at face value. It needs to be weighed. Motives of the source should be examined. Credibility should be assessed.

BURDEN OF PROOF

Here is one more important trial concept—the burden of proof. This is a basic concept about which side has the burden or obligation to prove an issue.

I spend most of my professional life as a plaintiff's lawyer. (In litigation, the person bringing the case is called the *plaintiff*.) That means that day in and day out, across the country, I go into courts before judges and juries to prove that my client has been wronged, that such wrong caused a damage, and that my client is entitled to recovery for that damage.

How is that done? I have what the law calls a *burden of proof*. I must prove certain things to allow my client to recover. If I am unable to prove my case, then my client loses. It is that simple.

Now while I am the lawyer for the aggrieved, called the *plaintiff's lawyer*, there is a lawyer for the party or parties on whom I am placing the blame. These lawyers are called *defense lawyers*. They defend those accused of wrongdoing. If I, as the plaintiff's lawyer, am unable to prove my case, if I am unable to carry my burden of proof, then the defense wins. The defense lawyer doesn't have to do anything at all to win if I haven't first proven my case.

In court there are special procedures built around this understanding. When presenting evidence and the case, the plaintiffs always go first. As the plaintiff's lawyer, I begin the trial using witnesses and documents to prove my case. After I "rest," it is the defense lawyer's turn. Before the defense lawyer starts, however, that lawyer can ask the judge to stop the case immediately, right in the middle, as it were. The defense lawyer stands up and asks the judge, "Your honor, the defense asks for a directed verdict." In other words, "Direct that the plaintiff loses because the plaintiff hasn't carried the burden of proof." If the plaintiff doesn't offer sufficient proof, the plaintiff loses. Game over.

Once the plaintiff has offered sufficient proof to allow one, if one chose to believe such evidence, to vote in favor of the plaintiff, then the defense puts on a case refuting the evidence of the plaintiff. Once all the evidence is in, the jury (or judge in certain cases), decides whether the evidence proves the plaintiff's case. This is the final decision of who wins, but even here, it is a question of whether the plaintiff has carried the burden of proof. Has the plaintiff proven her or his case?

Something important happens here. Enforcing the burden of proof means that some cases that are valid are still lost in a court of law. For example, if my case centers on Driver Dan running a red light and crashing into Plaintiff Patty, then I must prove Driver Dan ran the red light. Now Driver Dan might have actually run the red light, but I might not have any proof. Driver Dan might be dead and unable to testify. Plaintiff Patty might be in a coma and unable to testify. There might be no witnesses to testify. So I am left unable to carry the burden of proof, and I lose the case, even though actual historical events were that Driver Dan ran the red light.

Who has the burden of proof is key in any case. If I get to assume that Driver Dan ran the red light *unless Driver Dan can prove otherwise,* then I can win the case with no witnesses. Driver Dan would not be able to carry his burden of proof. Of course, in American courts, such is not the case. The plaintiff is required to prove the case first, not the defendant, although if the defendant is asserting their own affirmative contention, they may have a burden to prove that contention. The same principle is true in a criminal case. The state, through the prosecutor, has the burden of proof. The defendant is presumed innocent until proven guilty. In some cases, the defendant may truly *be* guilty, but without proof, even that defendant can go free.

The burden of proof will be important in this book. I have tried to bring together authentic and credible witnesses for the various issues under consideration. (So when I write up why atheists don't believe in God, I use atheist sources.)

American courts have evolved rules and procedures from over a thousand years of society's efforts to determine truth. These rules are the latest and greatest tools at hand for discerning important matters of life and liberty. Some of history's greatest minds have sculpted and refined these rules so that logic and common sense, when applied to properly handled evidence, can produce judgments worthy of society's confidence.

I will use that approach, use those rules of logic, common sense, and fair play, to examine the tenets of atheism, agnosticism, and scientific materialism. I do so admittedly from a Christian perspective, but not out of defensiveness for what I believe. I try to approach each argument to see if I might be wrong. I want truth. The courtroom gives me the best tools for finding that truth. So that is the scope of this project.

With this legal primer in place, and with appropriate explanations of methodology and my disclosure of personal faith, let me begin.

OPENING
STATEMENT

MAY IT PLEASE THE COURT:

Almost everyone desires to know and understand things beyond oneself. Humanity seems hard-wired for curiosity, but not in the same way as a cat. People seek out *information*, not simply *stimulation*. Some have termed humans as "informavores," substituting an appetite for information into a well-known word for eating (carnivores, herbivores, etc.).[1]

People consume information constantly, watching television, listening to news or sports, surfing web pages, reading books, and dialoguing with others. At its root, even gossip is seeking information—conversations, tabloids, and web pages are often laden with the latest on So-and-So.

Of course, people readily question and seek information greater than who is dating whom, or whose marriage is falling apart. Most people readily discuss or opine on big questions of life and existence. I love to ask people if they believe in extraterrestrial life. I am frequently stunned at how many people quickly profess a belief in ETs, while others are adamantly against the concept. Or try starting a conversation about whether global warming is a human driven event or simply cyclical. Ask folks about politics and who should get one's vote. People are informavores with opinions!

While these big questions haunt the minds of many and can be fertile fields for dialogue, perhaps the most consequential questions center on faith. Is there a God (or gods)? What religion, if any, deserves my allegiance? Is religious faith simply an opiate for the masses, à la Karl Marx?[2]

Many aren't as comfortable engaging in these discussions of faith or faithlessness. It is readily added to many lists of things not to discuss at the dinner table (generally along with politics and finances). Maybe this discussion is best in the isolation of a book. The key is to think through these things carefully. This information, and the decisions one makes, aren't superficial gossip. These questions are central to reality and truth in life. These are "first importance" matters.

As I frame these discussions, and as I set up my examination of atheism and agnosticism, I embrace a familiar mantra: if the shoe fits, wear it. The mantra is at home in stories, notably Cinderella. The glass slipper that left Cinderella's foot when fleeing the ball bespoke Cinderella as the rightful wearer because it fit only her foot. But the mantra is also famous in courtroom lore, as Johnnie Cochran successfully defended O. J. Simpson arguing that the murderer's gloves exonerated O. J. since they didn't fit his hand. "If the glove don't fit, you must acquit."[3]

The shoe-fit mantra applies to my views on life's biggest questions. I need this world to make sense. I need a view of the world that fits what I see, experience, and know in my life. If my view of the world (whether atheism, agnosticism, or belief in God) doesn't fit with the evidence of life, then I must stand ready to jettison my view. This drives my consideration about the issues in this book.

Some of these big questions arise out of how my mind works:

- Why do I think in terms of fairness? Why do I think what is fair is a worthy goal?
- Why do I believe that right and wrong in some areas isn't simply a matter of personal taste or opinion?
- Why do I believe that Black lives matter, Brown lives matter, women's lives matter, poor lives matter, sick lives matter, aged

lives matter—heavens, that any group being lessened or mistreated by society matters?

- Why do I value human life uniquely over that of the "other animals"?

Similar questions bother me about behavior:

- Why do I do things I don't want to do, even when they are destructive?

- Why do I fail to do things I want to do, even when they are clearly best?

For me these answers need to be part of a consistent worldview. My answers to one question can't be invalidated by my answer to another. On a simplified level, if you ask me why I ordered a turkey burger for lunch, it is okay for me to answer, "I don't eat red meat!" But then if the next meal you ask me why I ordered a ribeye steak for dinner, I better not answer, "Because I hate turkey." Those answers, each on its own, are fine. But when you put the two together, you find inconsistency.

In the same way, I am compelled to find answers to big questions that harmonize. I expect consistency. Consistency is a bedrock of logic, science, and sound thinking. I must have that consistency.

So as I examine the opinions of others for answers to life's questions, I am looking for uniformity of thought and logic. I am not satisfied when someone tells me something that doesn't make sense. Common sense may not always be right, but it should never be underrated.

Figure 2.1. Explanations for life's questions fall into different buckets

My examination of the explanation for life's questions falls into different buckets. The first bucket contains those who teach what I term *skeptical faiths* or *non-faiths*. This bucket considers whether those who adhere to atheism, agnosticism, or scientific materialism can give satisfactory and consistent answers to their views of existence and the world. Spoiler alert: I don't believe they do!

In fairness I should add that this book is a rather one-sided discussion. It is my dialogue with myself. But while I am not able to engage the reader directly, I hope to engage the reader fairly. In an actual trial, my opening statement would be one side of an understanding of truth followed by the other side's opening statement. Because I am unable to engage in the adversarial process of a true trial, I have tried to substitute the best thing. I have gleaned through arguments and explanations of world belief/unbelief systems by using the works of adherents of that system. I have tried to represent those systems fairly in assessing how they answer these big questions that I need answered for life to make sense. I have weighed those various answers in my own mind, assessing the evidence in favor of each, in coming to my own decisions about faith.

My examination of the second bucket considers various religions of the world. These will form the subject of an upcoming book, as I examine the world's most prominent religions for answers to life's pressing questions.[4]

These projects are part of a trilogy for my life's examination of faith. The first volume was published several years ago, where I cross-examined the Christian faith.[5] Because I am a Christian, I believe it proper to cross-examine Christianity, just as much as any other belief system.

I need to ascertain what view of reality and the cosmos best explains the condition of the world, of people, of me. In this volume, I examine philosophies of disbelief, and I will compare them to the system that at this point in my life makes the most sense to me. In consumer parlance, I need to determine if there is a better model. To make that decision, I first consider my current model.

For example, if I decide that I might want to buy a new car, and if I am doing so not simply because I am in the mood for a new one, but rather because I think I *need* a new one, then I first assess the car I have. Does it run? Does it run well? Does it have the features I want and need? Is it reliable? Does it need excessive maintenance? Is it economical to run? After I make these determinations, I can compare the newer model. Does it run better? Does it have better features? Does it make better economic sense? Is it safer?

This comparative approach means that I need to first set out my current belief system enough to make the comparison sensible. Because I believe the Christian faith best answers life's great questions in a consistent and logical manner, my Christian beliefs must take the stage first.

GOD

The formative Christian belief centers on the existence of a God as a spiritual being unlike anything one can know from the physical materials of the universe. This God exists independently of the physical universe. This God has a distinct and unchanging ethic/morality. God's morality puts limits on what he would or would not do.[6] Though not a person in a human sense, this God has a nature that humans can best label as *person*ality. (This is "language of accommodation," having to use human terms for the divine.[7])

God is infinite in time and scope. God is unchanging in his essential nature, being the same essential being yesterday, today, and tomorrow. God is responsible through creation of all that exists in this universe.

HUMANITY

God made humanity to work in this world with creativity, finding fulfillment and fellowship through a relationship with God. Humanity was hardwired by God to be moral also, reflecting and sharing in God's morality. While humanity was made to reflect God, the differences between God and humanity are huge (infinite vs. finite; without beginning and end vs. created and capable of death; beyond space and time vs. captive to space and time; self-sufficient and satisfied vs. dependent; etc.).

SIN

Humanity chose to rebel against God's morality and "fell," the biblical metaphor for becoming sinful, being driven by evil desires, being unable to achieve perfection, becoming unjust and prejudiced, and being less than one was made to be. This fallen humanity can no more coexist with a morally pure God in a relationship than a failed course can coexist with a perfect 4.0 GPA. You add an F to the 4.0 GPA, and the GPA is reduced. In like manner, you can't add sinful people to a united relationship with a sinless God.

SIN'S EFFECTS

God's justice and unchanging existence can only have the deep level of intimacy that humanity was made to have if humanity finds purity. Try as humans might, none can achieve God's purity. The life that humans live in sin must be put to death. A life in harmony with God must be based on purity or moral righteousness. The predicament between moral righteousness and fairness is at the root of many discussions of life because humanity recognizes deep in its core that there is a greater morality than people can possess, but people should strive for it nonetheless.

SCRIPTURE

God has revealed himself to humanity not only through Jesus but also through inspired Scriptures, placed into this world through the pens and mouths of God's prophets. These Scriptures reveal God truly, though not fully. In other words, the Bible teaches about God in true ways, but not exhaustive ways. While God has revealed all things necessary for people to enter into a relationship with him, that doesn't mean God is revealed exhaustively.

JESUS

There is only one God, but that one God exists in persons commonly known as the Father, Son, and Holy Spirit. This concept is generally termed the Trinity, from the Latin term meaning "three-ness." While God is not dependent on this universe, God has entered the universe through incarnation in space and time, becoming Jesus of Nazareth.

Jesus is fully God as well as fully human. Jesus existed in the full expression of God prior to the incarnation and birth of Jesus of Nazareth. Even after the Jesus' death and resurrection, Jesus still reigns as God. Jesus lived as the perfect expression of God in human form, living a pure sinless life of moral perfection and unbroken fellowship with God.

REDEMPTION

Humanity's cruelty was manifested through many around Jesus who killed his body in a real historical event, being crucified on a Roman cross under the aegis of Pontius Pilate. Through God's provision and in accord with divine justice, Jesus chose to bear the human responsibility and cost of sin and rebellion against God. The death justly deserved by impure humans was meted out in a cosmic and eternal sense in the death of Jesus the perfect one.

Through his life and death, Jesus ushered in the kingdom of God and a new creation, not yet fully realized in space and time. Humanity can place themselves into a right relationship with God—one that is just—when humanity accepts in faith and trust in the death of Jesus as the atonement for one's sins.

Jesus's human death was real, and so was his resurrection. The physical resurrection of Jesus is the hope of all who place themselves into a relationship with God based on the substitution of Jesus's death as our own punishment. For just as Jesus was raised to a new life, never to die again, so those who place their faith in God can look forward after death to a new life that will never end.

THE NOW AND THE NOT YET

Now Christians (those who place their trust in Jesus and claim his death for their own) are not orphaned on earth. God has chosen to dwell within the Christians' hearts through the Holy Spirit. In this sense, God is in the Christian, even as the Christian is in God through Christ. Those who have this relationship with God through Christ have a peace that is not found elsewhere. Part of that peace comes from being able to answer the big questions of life.

NONBELIEVERS

Absent a vibrant relationship with God, one will find a gnawing in one's heart, thinking that there must be something more to life. Christianity teaches that humanity was meant to walk in relationship with God, exercising dominion over the earth in accordance with God's will (i.e., responsibly!). Without that relationship, a gaping hole exists that people try to fill with everything from money, food, sex, power, popularity, mind-altering drugs and drink, and even self-denial and other supposed virtues. Yet only a vibrant walk with God yields the peace that humanity was made to experience. Nothing else.

Because people are hardwired with a drive to morality and meaning beyond daily existence, many people throughout history and the world have developed belief systems. Some believe in the existence of divinity; some believe there is no God (or gods). Both groups, however, evidence elements of truth as God's thumbprint remains upon them whether they realize it or not.

While many embrace various religions, many people are unbelievers in any concept of God. The underlying causes of unbelief may be disappointment in life, efforts to stifle one's own fears of meaninglessness or insignificance, an acute sense of how unfair life can be, a rebellion against God to make life heaven on earth (for example, to get rid of disease on command), or just a numbness to asking the questions about life with a sincere probing mind.

With this model set forth, I now begin to examine the other models to establish whether they are improvements on the answers to my questions about life. I want to prompt questions, probe alternative theories, and derive truthful answers. These answers to big questions of faith rightly break down into a multitude of other questions. These are questions of reality. What is truly real? That which is truly real should satisfactorily answer my big questions rooted in why I am the way I am, and why you are the way you are.

With unbelief on trial, let court commence.

ATHEISM AND THE BURDEN OF PROOF

I HAVE MORE THAN A FEW GOOD FRIENDS who describe them-selves as atheists. The idea that atheists are "godless, immoral com-munists" isn't my experience at all. I have found many atheists to be marvelous, ethical people of compassion.

To better understand atheism, I often ask those who describe them-selves as atheists, "When did you become an atheist?" Many grew up with no faith; there was no turning point where a faith was jettisoned. Very few of these are what I term *intellectual atheists*. By that I mean that very few are atheists truly because of intellectual reasons. Most may think they are, but when you get down to it, they aren't. They have just never processed the logic pro and con. They may have con-sidered the idea of God but dismissed it because their thoughts ulti-mately led nowhere.

There are also many atheists who don't want to believe in God. I've met more than a few who have decided not to believe in God out of hurt or anger. Some event or tragedy occurred, and such a one decides, "There surely isn't a God, or he would have prevented . . ." A few of this type might even believe in God deep down, but they refuse to admit so because they are punishing God for letting the tragedy occur. Generally, these are atheists who at an earlier stage in their lives would have said, "Yes, I believe in God."

Still others are atheists because of apathy toward the subject. These are folks whose lives are going fine, they have friends, they have jobs, they eat well, live in safety, and seem to have no need for God. When asked if they believe in God, they answer no, but when asked why, frequently can't or don't care to give an answer of much depth.

Very few of the atheists I have encountered have dug into the ideas and proofs of God and have then decided that the intellectually honest position is that there is no God. Even among these, however, many, if not most, still have a shallow grasp of the argument's pros and cons. They may have read a popular atheism book like Richard Dawkins's *The God Delusion*, but they haven't done much more than that.

In my examination of the atheistic position, I try to dig deeply into the reservoir of arguments for atheism. My goal is to try and fairly assess whether proof of atheism is compelling. Before I detail my considerations, let me clarify how I use several terms.

THEISM, ATHEISM, AND AGNOSTICISM

I repeatedly use these three terms: *theism*, *atheism*, and *agnosticism*. The words *atheism* and *agnosticism* can confuse people, yet each has an important and distinctive meaning.

Both *theism* and *atheism* come from the Greek word *theos*, the word for "god." In English, -*ism* is added to the end of a word to indicate a belief or something with which some agree. For example, *capitalism* is a belief in an economic system built around people keeping capital they generate. *Socialism* is a belief in an economic system structured on the social network, or community at large, receiving the benefits generated by the community at large. This same language construction principle is at work with the Greek word *theos* (θεός) or "god." So *theism* means "a belief in the existence of god or gods."

Ancient Greek had letters that they would use to attach to the beginning of words, affecting the word's meaning. English does similarly. In Greek, if one attached the letter *a* to the beginning of a word, it meant the negative of what would otherwise be meant. This is like the English prefixes *im-* or *un-*. In English, these letters function to turn the "possible" into the "impossible." It takes people who are "noticeable" and makes them "unnoticeable."

Using Greek, the letter *a* set before *theism* makes *atheism*. Since *theism* means "a belief in a god," *atheism* means "a belief that there is no god or gods." Some atheists dispute this definition. The American Atheists, Inc. website notes,

> Atheism is not an affirmative belief that there is no god, nor does it answer any other question about what a person believes. It is simply a rejection of the assertion that there are gods. Atheism is too often defined incorrectly as a belief system. To be clear: Atheism is not a disbelief in gods or a denial of gods; it is a lack of belief in gods.[1]

I am not out to challenge the American Atheists' definition of *atheism*. Under their definition, many of the arguments for or against atheism will fall under my chapters dealing with agnosticism. But from a linguistic perspective, and for many if not most people, atheism is different from agnosticism.

A similar definition is offered by English philosopher and atheist John Gray. In his book *Seven Types of Atheism*, he gives a provisional definition of atheism, noting, "I suggest that an atheist is anyone with no use for the idea of a divine mind that has fashioned the world. In this sense atheism does not amount to very much. It is simply the absence of a creator-god."[2] As Gray silos seven different atheisms, that which I call an atheist is generally found in his first or second grouping, either the "New Atheists: A Nineteenth-Century Orthodoxy" or "Secular Humanism, A Sacred Relic."

My intent in defining these terms is not to quibble with atheists over whether I use the term in the same way they might. My terms are explained and used only to make sense of how I process the arguments. To these atheists, and their positions, one must consider in tandem my chapters on agnosticism as well as atheism.

Agnosticism comes from the Greek word *gnosis* (γνῶσις), which denotes "knowing" or "knowledge."[3] When you attach the Greek *a* to the beginning of that word, you get *agnosticism* which means "a belief of uncertainty." As a system of uncertainty, agnosticism says, "I don't know if there's a god or not."[4]

So as I use a common linguistic approach, one who claims to be an atheist is claiming that there is no god(s). When someone claims to be an agnostic, one is claiming to be uncertain whether there is a god(s). When asked if God exists, the atheist says, "No." The agnostic says, "I don't know," or, "Not that I know of."

ATHEISM AND THE BURDEN OF PROOF

Many courthouses across America have sculptures or pictures of scales of justice. These are a physical feature that emphasize the process of just decision making. The idea is that to decide what is true and real, the decision-maker is to place the evidence into scales. Group the evidence for a position and the evidence against the position. Then put the evidence "for" on one side of the scales, while putting the contrary evidence on the other side of the scales. In this way, one properly weighs the evidence and decides truth.

Importantly, these scales also reflect the legal concept of proof. In most every civil case around the country, when I need to "prove" my case, the judge will instruct the jury that I do so, only when the evidence on one side of the scales outweighs the evidence on the other side. Proof is shown by the tilting of the scales. In language, this is frequently described as "the greater weight of the credible evidence."

Figure 3.1. The scales of justice emphasize the process of just decision making

Proof means different things to different disciplines. To a logician or philosopher, proof is determined by logic of inductive and deductive reasoning. Often it is expressed in mathematical formulas. A simplified example is:

For P ^ Q to be true, both P and Q must be true.

In this example, P represents a formula or a statement that is either true or false—like, "Mark Lanier is a trial lawyer" (which happens to be true). The inverted V (^) is a conjunction, or the formulaic equivalent of *and*. The capital Q is another formula or statement that can be true or false—like, "Mark Lanier is forty-five years old" (which happens to be false). To a logician, for P ^ Q to be true, that is, to prove that Mark Lanier is a forty-five-year-old trial lawyer, then *both* P and Q must be true. If either is untrue, one can be certain that the entire statement is untrue.

Proof to a medical researcher means something quite different. Certainty is almost unreachable for many medical questions. Consider whether a certain coronavirus vaccine works. The vaccine must be tested in a sufficiently large and diverse group of people at various doses. The results need to be tallied. Then one tries to determine to a degree of statistical significance what is the efficacy of the vaccine, if any. The researcher might say, "This vaccine works 97 percent of the time at doses of *x*." But even this statement of proven fact will generally be based on a 95 percent confidence interval. In other words, the researcher really means, "I am 95 percent certain that this vaccine works 97 percent of the time when given at this dose."

Proof to a chemist means even something different. If a chemist wants to know if a solution has an acidic or alkaline pH, then a piece of litmus paper can provide proof. Light blue litmus paper turns red under acidic conditions of a certain range or intensity. The litmus test is so clear that it has made it into general vocabulary as a test where a single factor is decisive.

Legal proof is distinct from other disciplines, even though it uses those disciplines. In a courtroom, I have many things to prove. For example, in 2018, I tried a case for twenty-two women who had suffered from ovarian cancer. My case was premised on these women's decades long use of asbestos-laced talc-based products causing their cancer. Among the things I had to prove were:

- The products had asbestos in them.
- The women used the products in question in a sufficient amount to put the asbestos into their bodies.
- Asbestos at the exposure levels of these ladies can cause ovarian cancer.
- Asbestos from the talc products was the cause of *their* ovarian cancer.

Those elements of proof combined disciplines of chemistry, minerology, medicine, statistics, and logic. The law required me to use proper levels of proof for *each* of those disciplines.

Yet that was not all I had to prove. In a case that ultimately made it to the United States Supreme Court,[5] I had to prove the damages to each lady. This wasn't simply "proving" each had cancer. It included whether there was pain and suffering that could be assessed a value in dollars and cents. Further, I had to prove that the defendant company *knew* the asbestos was present but recklessly and/or intentionally hid that fact. I had to prove *motive*. No science test, no logician's proof, no philosopher's tautology would prove motive or the economic value of pain. It took a whole different type of proof.

Ultimately in that trial, the jury made its assessment based on what the evidence proved to be true. The judge charged the jury to weigh all the evidence, assign weight based on the evidence's credibility, and then see if I "carried the burden of proof." By that the judge meant, Did the greater weight of credible evidence support each element I had to prove? If it did, my clients won. If it didn't—if I failed to carry my burden to prove the truth—then we lost. (We did win, by the way.)

Using legal proof, I have sought to find if atheism can be proven true. As I research, assess the evidence and arguments, and measure the credibility, am I persuaded? When I put the credible evidence for atheism on one side of the scales and then I put the credible evidence against atheism on the other, how do the scales tilt?

Whether or not I embrace atheism, the key for me, as well as a jury, is to avoid letting bias affect my verdict. As fairly as I might, I need to ask whether atheism adequately convinces me of its truth, as I view through the prism of the reality I find in this world, its people, and me.

EVIDENCE FOR ATHEISM

For evidence in favor of the position there is no God, I first went to the most vocal and popular among the proponents of a movement often termed *the new atheism*. In the early twenty-first century, four voices came forth and were often labeled "the Four Horsemen of the New Atheism." They are Sam Harris, Richard Dawkins, Daniel Dennett, and the now-deceased Christopher Hitchens. Each of these gentlemen wrote bestselling books asserting their atheism with an almost evangelistic fervor.

I selected their books to see how the prophets of atheism go about proving their belief God does not exist. I wanted to list their evidence against the existence of God on one side of the scales to compare it to the evidence for the existence of God. I read Richard Dawkins claim, "faith is belief in the teeth of evidence," and I wanted to see that evidence.[6] I wanted them to carry their burden of proof and tilt the scales, showing me why reason dictates there is no God.

I also tried to assess their credibility individually, as well as the credibility of their arguments. Several of them have some impressive credentials, and to an untrained eye, their writings might seem persuasive. But looking through a legal lens, I came away disillusioned and somewhat frustrated.

I then probed the less popular but more thoughtful (to me) atheists like John Gray (*Straw Dogs* and *Seven Types of Atheism*) and Thomas Nagel (*The Last Word*). These thinkers seem to recognize, and even address, the concerns and shortcomings I have found in the Four Horsemen, but their reasons still fail to sustain any burden of proof. In fact, Gray concurs with much of my thought in his challenges to Dawkins and his ilk, terming their approach "pseudo-science," explaining their popular approach "a relic of the nineteenth-century philosophy of Positivism."[7]

Finally, I went to the internet, admittedly a bit sophomoric, yet a source for many. I wanted to see how the most substantive and prominent websites argue that there is no God. The arguments on the internet were less developed than the books. But these were valuable arguments nonetheless. They are many of the arguments in daily discourse.

I came away from the books and websites disappointed. As a lawyer living in courtrooms, every case depends on proof. As I put forward an argument in court, I must prove it. No one offers much real credible proof there is no God. Most spend their energy haranguing against religion and its errors, asserting that faith exists in a region of the mind (which, of course is just as true for belief that there is no God), and they did so using logical fallacies and rhetorical devices, one right after the other.

CAN YOU PROVE A NEGATIVE?

Some argue that you can't prove a negative. Those people haven't spent time in a courtroom! "Proof" in the sense of convincing a reasonable mind is not difficult. I explain this in more detail later, but I could fairly prove that there is no elephant in my driveway, if in fact there was none. I would marshal proof of what an elephant is, including its size and physical/material attributes; I would establish that my driveway is fully visible and would show such a creature; I would establish that a group of people with good eyesight and investigatory abilities inspected the driveway during the relevant time frame; that each could independently confirm that there is no place where an elephant as defined would not be visible, and yet none was seen. I would then have adequate proof for a reasonable mind to fairly conclude that no elephant is in my driveway.

The books do not offer any substantive proof that God doesn't exist, at least not in the sense of what a court would consider. At best, they tear down reasons for believing in God. Those are two vastly different things. Let me explain with a red-light example.

Suppose a lawyer in court argues that Driver Dan ran a red light and hit Plaintiff Patty. Trying to prove the case, the lawyer produces an eyewitness, Blind Betty. Blind Betty takes the stand and testifies that she saw Driver Dan run a red light. Then the defense attorney begins cross-examination and proves that Blind Betty was not wearing her glasses at the time. Blind Betty clearly wasn't reliably able to see the color of the light.

Now, the defense attorney may have destroyed the eyewitness evidence, but that doesn't mean that Driver Dan didn't run the red light. He might have or might not have. All that has happened thus far is the lawyer has yet to prove it. So it is with these preachers of atheism. They are good at attacking certain aspects of religion and belief, but they never offer rational or substantive proof that there is no God.

A prime example is Richard Dawkins. Dawkins doesn't prove his atheism; he simply has faith in his worldview and works to shift the burden of proof. Dawkins hit the bestseller lists and made substantial money selling his book *The God Delusion*. The book presents itself as detailed analysis dispelling the myth of God and proving atheism.

Dawkins produces an entire chapter that makes one think, "*I am finally going to get the proof there is no God!*" The chapter is titled, "Why There Is Almost Certainly No God." The problem is the chapter doesn't offer any proof on why there is almost certainly no God. Instead, the chapter works to destroy the views of creationism and intelligent design, while setting forth classical evolution as an explanation of origins. That is not proof there is no God.

There are countless Christian believers who subscribe to the belief that the Bible is not to be read as a science book. Many incredibly focused and credentialed bedrock Christian scholars have explained that reading Genesis (the book of the Old Testament with the clearest creation story) in its historical context should *not* be read as a science book.[8] Any serious reader of the Bible must recognize that the translation chore is not only getting the ancient Hebrew, Aramaic, and Greek into modern language but also translating the ancient culture and knowledge into modern understanding. So many Bible believers recognize that the biblical God could have set the knobs for the cosmos to unfold as it has. Therefore, evolution, true or not, is not proof that there is no God.

Dawkins also sets out another reason there is "no God" in the chapter. His alternate reason is that the universe is so big, and its component parts are so small, a God capable of handling such would be too massive to conceive.

A God capable of continuously monitoring and controlling the individual status of every particle in the universe cannot be simple. His existence is going to need a mammoth explanation in its own right. Worse (from the point of view of simplicity), other corners of God's giant consciousness are simultaneously preoccupied with the doings and emotions and prayers of every single human being—and whatever intelligent aliens there might be on other planets in this and 100 billion other galaxies.[9] I can surmise from this that God's "mind" would have to be a lot bigger than Richard Dawkins's mind (or yours or mine). Bigger than even a computer!

God may not have a brain made of neurons, or a CPU made of silicon, but if he has the powers attributed to him, he must have something far more elaborately and nonrandomly constructed than the largest brain or the largest computer we know.[10]

With all due respect to Richard Dawkins's brain power, that is not proof there is no God. If the average human brain is a full three pounds of grey matter, and I give Dawkins a brain and a half, still even four and a half pounds of neural and glial cells surely cannot be the standard for determining the makeup of the mind of God. I suspect that an ant could probably never conceive in that small ant mind, that some being exists who can put a rocket on Mars. For that matter, I doubt the ant can even contemplate Mars.

This is a classic illustration of the arguing fallacy of a straw man. In a courtroom, one would rise and say, "Objection, calls for facts not in evidence." In other words, Dawkins is implying, if not explicitly saying, that God must be considered as a superhuman with a superbrain, or a supercomputer. Dawkins is making his readers think in those terms. That makes it a bit absurd to believe in God, if one is trying to make him into a larger version of what people are or what people create.

But if God is not a human being, even a super-sized one; if God is not of the human race at all; if God is an entity or essence far beyond what humans are; if God is not made of the substance of this universe, then Dawkins is still left without any proof such a God doesn't exist. Dawkins returns to the world of those who must shift the burden of proof, like so many others I discuss.[11]

If one tries to chase down notable intellectuals in recent history who have written for atheism, one quickly comes across the writings of popular astronomer Carl Sagan (1934–1996) and the British philosopher Bertrand Russell (1872–1970). Both are famous for their "proofs" that there is no God. Sagan published an essay, "The Dragon in My Garage," as chapter ten in his book *The Demon-Haunted World— Science as a Candle in the Dark* (1996). People often reference this illustration to show that there can be no proof of God, as well as why it is absurd to think God exists. Sagan used it in the chapter to argue against alien abduction, but the metaphor is larger than aliens. Many use it to argue that it is okay to fully discount something that can never be scientifically proven.

Here is a synopsis of it. One says, "A fire-breathing dragon exists in my garage." As the hearer challenges that truth, an excuse is given for each challenge or attempted proof. When the hearer says, "Let me look in your garage," he is told, "The dragon is invisible." When the hearer says, "I will spray paint and make him visible," he is told, "No, he is also incorporeal." The hearer wants to try infrared sensors for the fire but is told the fire isn't hot so won't show up on the sensors. On and on the metaphor goes, and at the end, the reader is left with the analogy of trying to prove that "an invisible, incorporeal, floating dragon who spits heatless fire" doesn't exist. That can't be done.

Using Sagan's analogy to prove atheism is a subtle attempt to shift the burden of proof. His metaphor works to say, "I don't have to prove there is no God. If you can't prove there is a God, then it is acceptable to say he doesn't exist." But this is not a valid analogy to use on whether atheism is provable or proven. This shifting burden of proof sounds good, because it inherently equates believing in God to believing in a dragon, or even worse, in an "an invisible, incorporeal, floating dragon who spits heatless fire." All because it cannot be proven with scientific technique or direct evidence.

Notably, even with a shifting burden of proof, the lawyer in me still takes issue with the faulty way Sagan has his hearer go about trying to prove the dragon exists. If the person was first tied down to what a dragon is, then the proof is much simpler. In other words, get the language precise. If the person agrees to the first definition of the *Oxford English Dictionary*, then a dragon is "a huge serpent or snake; a python." This then becomes testable. It can no longer be an "invisible, incorporeal, floating dragon who spits heatless fire." If someone uses the *OED*'s second definition, then one has a "mythical monster, represented as a huge and terrible reptile, usually combining ophidian and crocodilian structure, with strong claws, like a beast or bird of prey, and a scaly skin; it is generally represented with wings, and sometimes as breathing out fire."[12] This too becomes testable.

If the dragon owner refuses the Oxford dictionary definition, have the person come up with his or her own. The owner may tell you the dragon is a metaphor for anxiety in life, in which event, the owner may be right! Such a dragon might indeed exist! The owner may be referencing *Game of Thrones* episodes with Daenerys Targaryen, mother of dragons, thinking that the dragons on the video count as dragons in the garage. In that event, the owner may indeed have that dragon. Either way, it is testable.

To show the fallacy of a Sagan-esque approach, instead of using a dragon, take something that is truly incorporeal. Think of the interpretation of Woody Guthrie's classic "This Train Is Bound for Glory." Guthrie died in 1967, so I don't have him to tell me what the train means. If I want to assert that the train bound for glory is liberation of the poor, then you could rightly ask me, How do you know? What are your reasons for thinking so? Can I just say, well, you can't prove I am wrong, so it must be what I say? Of course not.

I would need to marshal reasonable evidence from which the inference could be made.

Why, then, can someone say, "I believe the evidence shows there is no God, but the evidence is a lack of evidence until you prove he exists." God, as most people understand him, is not a corporeal being. Unlike Oxford's (and most everyone else's) definition of a dragon, God is not a creature of nature. No one can anymore prove him by tests that prove creatures of nature than one will prove the interpretation of a song by a corporeal test.

Consider the analogy of measurements. If I want to measure the amount of liquid in my medium Chick-fil-A Diet Dr Pepper, I could do so in ounces or some metric equivalent like milliliters. But I would be hard pressed to give you the amount of liquid using Fahrenheit or Centigrade numbers. Fahrenheit and Centigrade measure, but they don't measure the volume of liquids. They measure temperatures, whether of liquids, solids, or gasses.

Trying to prove or disprove the existence of a God who is allegedly outside of nature (or beyond nature, i.e., super to nature or "supernatural") by using the tools of nature's science is using the wrong measuring mechanism. People trying to use science to prove or disprove God's existence are making an assumption that is never really explored. The assumption is that science would detect the presence of a supernatural God. Absent God taking a physical form and then proving himself (something many eyewitnesses reported happened in Jesus), you will not have direct evidence of God, but instead circumstantial evidence.

Now that doesn't mean that one must write off the idea of proving God exists or doesn't exist. It just means that one needs to use the right tools. The tools of nature's science won't ever prove the depth of one's love for another, but that doesn't mean that love doesn't exist. The tools of science don't prove the meaning of a poem, but that doesn't mean the poem doesn't have meaning. The tools of science don't prove what is right and wrong, but right and wrong exist.

Certain people called to prove their atheism find Sagan's metaphor useful. Yet it isn't useful because it rightly assesses the evidence. It doesn't. It is useful to them because they can use Sagan's metaphor as a way of shifting the burden of proof from those who wish to assert there is no God. When used in that sense, the metaphor becomes a dodge, plain and simple. It becomes tantamount to an admission that there is no proof that God doesn't exist, under the guise of saying, "The proof he doesn't exist is that no one can prove he does exist."

Here is a simple example of this faulty logic. I cannot prove whether there is an even number of stars or an odd number of stars. Humanity doesn't even remotely know how many stars exist. But just because I can't prove whether the stars number out to an even or odd number, doesn't mean that they don't. The number of stars must be even or odd. That is the nature of numbering anything—even or odd. But that I can't prove the number as even or odd could never be taken as proof that the number is neither. One either needs to offer real proof there is no God, or move to what I term agnosticism, saying, "I genuinely don't know if a God exists," adding perhaps, "I strongly suspect or believe he doesn't!"

An argument like Sagan's is found in the writings of Bertrand Russell. Russell was a brilliant thinker and logician. He was also an atheist. Richard Dawkins writes approvingly of Russell's "parable of the celestial teapot."[13] Russell knew that there was great difficulty in proving his atheism, so he was an early one who attempted to shift the burden of proof. Russell wanted to make someone prove the existence of God, rather than him be forced to logically prove there is no God. Russell argued the shifting of the burden based on a tea kettle analogy:

> If I were to suggest that between the Earth and Mars there is a china teapot revolving about the sun in an elliptical orbit, nobody would be able to disprove my assertion provided I were careful to add that the teapot is too small to be revealed even by our most powerful telescopes. But if I were to go on to say that, since my

assertion cannot be disproved, it is intolerable presumption on the part of human reason to doubt it, I should rightly be thought to be talking nonsense. If, however, the existence of such a teapot were affirmed in ancient books, taught as the sacred truth every Sunday, and instilled into the minds of children at school, hesitation to believe in its existence would become a mark of eccentricity and entitle the doubter to the attentions of the psychiatrist in an enlightened age or of the Inquisitor in an earlier time.[14]

This analogy would likewise not hold up to a careful cross-examination in a court room.

First, if one were to assert there is a china teapot circling the sun in orbit, a careful cross-examination would reveal whether this is likely so. I would ask:

Q. On what basis do you believe this?

Getting an answer would then enable one to carefully define terms: exactly what is meant by a china teapot? Assuming one agrees that a china teapot is made of carefully fitted pieces of certain kind of clay that has been molded into a certain shape (with a handle and spout), fired at a certain temperature, then cooled off and placed into service, the next line of questions continues:

Q. On what basis do you believe there is that certain kind of clay?

Q. On what basis do you believe the clay was sculpted?

These questions would continue until reaching the issue of how the china tea kettle got into orbit.

If one should answer those questions sufficiently, adding perhaps that the tea kettle was placed into orbit by a cosmonaut on a space walk with a great sense of humor, then maybe the examination takes a different tack ("Who was the cosmonaut?"). If the answers are inadequate, then the natural follow-up questions might center around, "How did you come by this information?"

Now if I am looking for scientific proof of whether this tea kettle is in orbit, then perhaps no one will be able to prove it—the one asserting it or the one refuting it. It is silly. It is like measuring my Diet Dr Pepper with a speedometer rather than in ounces. But if I use a proper measuring approach, one like in a court of law and its evidence rules, then I can come to a reasonable area of proof. If one wants to disprove the tea kettle, it can be done—no psychiatrist or inquisition needed.

People thinking through this must remember that humanity lives in an orderly world, not a Harry Potter world of magic. As an orderly world of nature, there are ways of determining what exists in nature. Sometimes one can prove something exists. Sometimes one cannot prove it but still suspects it. Sometimes one can prove it doesn't exist. Those are claims of certain physical things of nature. Even those claims, however, take on a different form if one changes what one is searching for.

For example, if I want to assert that Caesar's invasion of Gaul in 49 BC was a real campaign, that it really happened in history, I would not be able to do so by the rules of science. Similarly, if one refuted the existence of that invasion, one could not disprove that. Should one refusing it simply be able to say, "Since you can't prove it, I assume it didn't happen?" Of course not. Like with the Woody Guthrie song, or the depth of my love for my wife and children, just because one cannot prove it with scientific certainty, doesn't mean something is not real. In like manner, should anyone *logically* think that the rules of science would detect the presence of a supernatural God? I am not surprised to find "circumstantial evidence" of him, but scientific evidence? Of course not.

Within that framework, the arguments to prove atheism thin out. I address those arguments next.

4

ATHEIST
ARGUMENTS

CHILDREN OFTEN DISTILL COMPLICATED MATTERS to their essence. One illustration of that truth that makes me chuckle is watching two children debate over a point. The debate might go something like:

Child 1: "My dad is stronger than your dad!"

Child 2: "No he isn't!"

Child 1: "Is too!"

Child 2: "Is not!"

Child 1: "Is too!"

This goes on for a while until Child 2 finally says, "Prove it!" Then the final stroke of brilliance as Child 1 replies, "No, *you* prove it." That back and forth then continues until the children tire.

The children are discussing the burden of proof. As I indicated in the last chapter, the courtroom takes the burden of proof away from such childish discourse by setting up rules. Whichever party has a substantive claim they wish to get as a finding generally has the burden to prove that claim. If Johnny sues Sue for a car wreck, Johnny must prove the wreck was Sue's fault. Johnny has the burden of proof. If Johnny fails to prove it, he loses. Sue doesn't have to prove anything. If, however, Sue knows it was her fault for hitting Johnny, but she wants to blame Henry for running into her first, Sue has the burden to prove Henry was at fault.

Many who espouse the atheist view try to shift the burden of proof from proving there is no God onto the shoulders of one who doesn't agree. It is the playground equivalent of, "No, you prove it!" Some atheists, however, produce certain arguments that seem to be substantive efforts at establishing a worldview of "There is no God" as true. I want to address those arguments uniquely set forward by notable atheists in this chapter.

When assessing these arguments, I have come to divide the proponents into two basic camps. For better or worse, and not meaning to be pejorative, those camps are popular writers and more ivory-tower writers. That is, some write for the common reader while others write more for academia. But points are learned by examining all of them.

As I examine these arguments, one thing that seems to arise over and over is a rhetorical sleight of hand. It is the arguer's equivalent of a magician's distraction that keeps you from seeing the trick performed under your not-so-watchful eyes. This device takes the form of logical fallacies. It gives an illusion of making sense, but once the trick (or fallacy) is exposed, the deception ends. Logical fallacies are not always easy to detect, especially to the untrained eye. They are optical illusions of the mind. They fool you and can be very deadly at persuading you to accept an illogical viewpoint. I read the books of the four horsemen and found them to be textbooks for logical fallacies.

Take as an example Sam Harris's book *The End of Faith*. Harris uses many textbook examples of logical fallacies in skewing his concepts of religion, all the while never offering substantive arguments or proof that God doesn't exist. The nonexistence of God is his default. His argument is not based on any substantive reason other than his disdain for his perceptions of religion. Even there, however, his reasoning is a good textbook to source for examples of logical fallacies.

If I were to put *The End of Faith* and Harris under the scrutiny of cross-examination, the logical fallacies of his magician's sleight of hand in attempting to end faith and foster atheism would be readily revealed. Consider his first chapter, titled "Reason in Exile." This chapter is a key to understanding his atheism. He believes that the reasons for believing a god exists are all fallacious; therefore, he posits, there must be no god.

I have demonstrated the logical problem with this reasoning, using Driver Dan and the red-light example. But with Harris it's worse than that. He claims that those who believe in God have sent their reasoning ability into exile. In fact, "Reason in Exile" more aptly describes Harris's own argumentation. Here are my legal objections to some of the logical fallacies Harris blithely dances across the pages.

AD HOC RESCUE, APPEAL TO EMOTION, AND RELEVANCE

These fallacies typically arise when someone desperately wants to believe or support a position but has no evidence. So when there is a problem with the position, one makes up an alternate reason to justify the unsupported position. This may seem complicated, but it isn't. Let me explain.

Harris doesn't support his belief that there is no God by proof of his nonexistence. Surely knowing that, Harris tries to unfold his arguments by attempting to destroy faith in religious beliefs. First, Harris makes up facts to cover his error in reasoning (an ad hoc rescue). For example, Harris tries to point to religion as the cause of human atrocity. He concocts a chilling story of a religious zealot blowing up a bus. Here is his effort:

> The young man boards the bus as it leaves the terminal. He wears an overcoat. Beneath his overcoat, he is wearing a bomb. His pockets are filled with nails, ball bearings, and rat poison.
>
> The bus is crowded and headed for the heart of the city. The young man takes his seat beside a middle-aged couple. He will wait for the bus to reach its next stop. The couple at his side

appears to be shopping for a new refrigerator. The woman has decided on a model, but her husband worries that it will be too expensive. He indicates another one in a brochure that lies open on her lap. The next stop comes into view. The bus doors swing. The woman observes that the model her husband has selected will not fit in the space underneath their cabinets. New passengers have taken the last remaining seats and begun gathering in the aisle. The bus is now full. The young man smiles. With the press of a button, he destroys himself, the couple at his side, and twenty others on the bus. The nails, ball bearings, and rat poison ensure further casualties on the street and in the surrounding cars. All has gone according to plan.

The young man's parents soon learn of his fate. Although saddened to have lost a son, they feel tremendous pride at his accomplishment. They know that he has gone to heaven and prepared the way for them to follow. He has also sent his victims to hell for eternity. It is a double victory. The neighbors find the event a great cause for celebration and honor the young man's parents by giving them gifts of food and money.

These are the facts . . . Why is it so easy, then, so trivially easy—you-could-almost-bet-your-life-on-it easy—to guess the young man's religion?[1]

Look at this story objectively and critically. Notice how Harris makes up details to increase your pity. This is a typical logical fallacy found in arguments (labeled an *appeal to emotions*). In courtrooms, the judge would give an instruction to the jury not to let sympathy play a part in their decision, and anyone who was so tied to sympathy that they could not fairly follow the judge's instruction would be excused and not allowed to serve on the jury. These appeals to emotion are notorious for confusing a real logical and evidence-based argument.

A trial lawyer's ears perk up to a likely "appeal to emotion" whenever an opposing advocate begins including details that are irrelevant to the real argument (a "relevance" fallacy). Irrelevant facts in Harris's made-up story include his personalizing of the family that gets blown up. "The couple at his side appears to be shopping for a new refrigerator. The woman has decided on a model, but her husband worries that it will be too expensive. He indicates another one in a brochure that lies open on her lap."[2]

Obviously, the refrigerator and brochure have nothing to do with the argument being made. Their function is to engage the reader, make the reader more appalled at the story, and elevate the reader's emotional response. This is not a logical argument; it is an emotional manipulation in the guise of an argument.

APPEAL TO INSTINCT, OVERGENERALIZATION, AND ASSUMING FACTS NOT IN EXISTENCE

After giving the story, Harris makes an absurd deduction that has no logical basis. It is a textbook illustration of the logical fallacy often called "appeal to instinct" as well as a fallacy of "overgeneralization." Harris says, referring to the young man who blew himself up along with the bus, "Why is it so easy, then, so trivially easy—you-could-almost-bet-your-life-on-it easy—to guess the young man's religion?"[3]

Of course, this is an appeal not only to instincts but to prejudices. Students of history will find other examples of people who kill others, and even themselves in the process, without religion as the drawing card. Harris hopes to keep the reader from realizing this, however, by making a factually incorrect error, asserting it as commonplace knowledge: "A glance at history, or at the pages of any newspaper, reveals that ideas which divide one group of human beings from another, only to unite them in slaughter, generally have their roots in religion."[4]

It is notable that all these logical fallacies are found in the first three substantive pages of chapter one. Why are they there? It seems that reading this is supposed to leave the reader concerned. "Oh no," the reader is to think, "religion is a bad thing!"

This stinging start to Harris's book works subtly to make the reader alarmed that unthinking adherence to religion is destructive, that religious zeal is dangerous, and that religious commitment leads to the atrocities of history. Harris is laying a fallacious groundwork to destroy one's faith. Harris wants his reader to think that faith is not a good thing after all.

The fallacy of this logic is clearly demonstrated by a fair and reasonable assessment of evidence, not concocted stories. Here is a better construction of the *whole* truth, without the coloring of his alarmism, fallacious reasoning, and one-sided presentation.

Religion can indeed be destructive. History has shown this. It can destroy, deface, detract, and hurt society, culture, individual growth, and more. Religion can also be constructive. History has shown this as well. It can build, beautify, enrich, and contribute to society, culture, individual growth, and more.

A good illustration of points one and two above is the history of slavery in the United States. People abused religion and religious thinking to support slavery. This was found among some of those who claimed a Christian faith.[5] This is point one. Yet it was also the religious people who led to the abolition of slavery. The principal abolitionist of Britain's slave trade was the devout Christian William Wilberforce, who famously wrote in his diary on October 28, 1787, "God Almighty has set before me two great objects, the suppression of the Slave Trade and Reformation of Morals."[6]

The great Protestant preacher Charles Spurgeon called slavery "the foulest blot."[7] Methodist church founder John Wesley wrote a tract condemning slavery in 1774, taking slave traders to task based upon God and religious belief:

> May I speak plainly to you? I must. Love constrains me: Love to *you*, as well as to those you are concerned with. Is there a GOD? you know there is. Is He a just GOD? Then there must be a state of retribution: A state wherein the just GOD will reward every

man according to his works. Then what reward will he render to
you? O think betimes! Before you drop into eternity! Think now,
He shall have judgment without mercy, that shewed no mercy.[8]

This is point two. Religion has proven itself valuable.

That religion has worked positively and negatively is nothing new
or surprising. Even in the times of the New Testament, the apostle Paul
wrote of his concern that evil would masquerade as good (2 Cor 11:14).
Similarly, Jesus spoke of wolves in sheep's clothing (Mt 7:15). Evil exists.
Good exists. You find both within religion and both outside religion.
That brings up the next error in Harris's exposition on this point.

Harris is just plain wrong.

If you were to look up the major killings in the twentieth century,
deemed by most as the bloodiest of all centuries, the debate would rage
over who was responsible for the most killed: Adolf Hitler, Joseph
Stalin, or Mao Zedong. If any of those strike you as a religious man,
then you might dig a little deeper.

Some argue Hitler was religious because of some of his references
to religion and God in public speeches.[9] One wonders if these people
really believe everything a politician says in public. If you read Hitler's
private table conversations written up by his secretary, you see Hitler's
mockery of the Christian faith. For example, on the nights of July 11-12,
1941, Hitler said, "The heaviest blow that ever struck humanity was
the coming of Christianity."[10] Later, on October 14, 1941, Hitler
said, "The best thing is to let Christianity die a natural death. . . .
Gradually the myths crumble."[11]

Setting aside Hitler, one can consider Joseph Stalin. Stalin is credited
with killing a minimum of twenty million people.[12] As with Hitler, there
is a deep reach by many with an atheistic worldview to dispel the idea
that Stalin became an atheist in his life. The definitive biography of
Stalin as of World War II was by Yemelyan Yaroslavsky (1878–1943).
Yaroslavsky quoted Stalin stating in 1940, "You know, they are fooling
us, there is no God . . . all this talk about God is sheer nonsense."[13]

Yaroslavsky doubtlessly had a good idea of what Stalin meant. Yaroslavsky led the Communist party's League of the Militant Godless. He led the atheistic efforts for much of communist Russia.

Here's the importance of this from a logical perspective. If Harris's reasoning is right—if a story that sadly kills several people shows that religion is bad and there is no God—then the twentieth century must prove there is a God! For the greatest tragic deaths occurred at the hands of atheists.

But alas, Harris's logical fallacies cannot properly be used to prove the existence of God. One cannot definitively say that Hitler, Stalin, Mao, or other historical figures are responsible for the greatest numbers of deaths because they were atheists. That may be true, or it may not be true. My key takeaway is that the facts clearly disprove the justification of Harris and others who claim that religious faith has brought about the atrocities of humanity.

It is possible to continue to take apart the writings of Harris, but these formative pages of his book bring forth typical issues with using him to prove there is no God. As I examine the writings of the other horsemen, I find the same intrinsic flaws. If I were to place them into the scales of evidence, they boil down to a few basic arguments, though in different permutations.

Beyond the popular books of these notable authors are several written by more carefully thought-out atheists. Among these I include John Gray. Gray correctly chastises those atheists who use the values and meaning that were historically found in faith, even while abandoning the faith that infused those values and meaning with substance. Gray doesn't spend his energies trying to argue there is no God; he just accepts it. While Gray effectively argues that the popular Dawkins-type atheists are really no more than moral "positivists," Gray himself will fall guilty of being an "unbelieving positivist."

Before dealing with those thoughtful responses of those like Gray, it is useful to consider the dearth of arguments that populate the websites and conversations with those who claim to have valid proofs there is no God. These aren't typically proofs in a logical or classical sense, much less a courtroom. Books like those of Dawkins and others have been carefully written and edited, hopefully with an eye toward making a critical improvement on the table of ideas in publication. In contrast, the internet isn't generally trying to add to the table of ideas. It, like general dinner conversations, more reflect what people are thinking rather than a well-reasoned publishable discourse.

While many of these websites' "proofs of atheism" are not technically offering proofs of any kind, I consider these arguments because they become popular. These are the discussion points people may have around the water cooler or with their neighbors.

"I don't see him." This is not a classical proof of anything. It assumes way too much. It assumes the person knows what to look for. It assumes it is possible to see God, that he is a visible being in our space, time, and dimension. It assumes God wants you to see him visually.

Consider what is happening when you see something. Science teaches that light is a stream of photons, massless packets of energy traveling through space very fast (at the speed of light). When the photon streams, also called electromagnetic radiation, hit the human eye, they pass through the front clear part called the cornea. Then they traverse through the pupil (the black dot in your eyeball), pass through the lens and into the back of the eye to light-sensitive tissue called the retina. It is there that special cells convert the light or photons into electrical signals that travel via the optic nerve into your brain, which makes sense of the photons.

Now, to speak of seeing something or someone, consider that the streaming photons called light generally hits other matter before entering one's pupil. When the light/photons hit matter (atoms, molecules, ions), then some of the photons are absorbed while others are reflected. The reflected ones enter the eye, giving the color of what wasn't reflected. Some point out that black is not a color because it is really an absence of all color, so no color is reflected to enter a pupil.

So when someone says, "I don't see God," what one is really saying is, "There is no matter in front of me reflecting the protons streaming around me into my eye!"

Well, is this surprising? Of course, there are lots of things I don't see. That doesn't mean they don't exist. I don't see ultraviolet radiation, which is streaming light of a different wavelength than the human eye can detect. I don't see love. I don't see oxygen. I don't see light waves as waves. I don't technically see the color of an item, I see the reflection of a spectrum of light that an item doesn't absorb. Of course, if God is incorporeal, one could not possibly see him in his true state.

Additionally, one can fairly ask in what manner the one asserting "I don't see him" has looked for him. Does one consider that maybe in seeing the order and structure of the cosmos, one sees God? Perhaps the nonphysical God is seen in the people he indwells, should he in fact do so.

This argument is not proof there is no such thing as God; it is the cry of one who wants a corporeal God to touch, smell, or sense in some way. If this is an excuse for people to justify not believing in God, I find it very inadequate. If it is an earnest plea for God to show himself as real, I urge people to consider that he has, in ways that exceed electric impulses from the back of the eyeball!

"I don't feel him." Like the argument of not seeing God, this proof assumes too much. First, there is the assumption that God can be sensed or felt. Do the people asserting this proof have a belief in extra-sensory perception (ESP)? Can they sense things like God? How would they know if they were sensing God, or whether it was merely indigestion from a bad burrito? Would they accept it as proof of God if someone else said, "I sense him"? Because plenty of people say that. Not sensing God is not proof of whether he is there or isn't. Too many assumptions must be proven before the conclusion can be drawn that there is no God.

At its root, this is often more a complaint than an argument. Life teaches everyone that feelings come and go. Even as a believer in God,

I readily admit there are days when I feel him more than other days. Some might be stunned to read in the Bible that the Psalms, those poems that speak deeply from the human soul, recount times where the writer doesn't sense God. "How long, O LORD? Will you forget me forever? How long will you hide your face from me?" (Ps 13:1).

To those who don't sense God, I urge them to spend time seeking his presence. Pray for his truth. Find songs to sing to him. This may seem absurd to an unbeliever, but if so, then the unbeliever needs to find a different argument than not sensing God.

"There is no Zeus either." This irks me because it assumes there is no Zeus. Personally, I don't believe Zeus exists, but it still bothers me that someone simply makes that assumption, and then uses that assumption as proof there is no God. I will grant there is no Zeus in the sense that the ancient Greeks believed the head of the pantheon sat on Mount Olympus. But that doesn't mean there is no God. The two are not related. In the vernacular of argumentation logic, this fallacy could be termed a *non sequitur*. The two do not follow one from the other.

There is a massive and complicated scholastic understanding of why belief in the Greek/Roman pantheon of gods died out. It involves considerations of the logic of the limitations painted with such gods, the recognition that monotheism made more philosophical sense, the supplanting of polytheism with Christian thought, and more.

To say that Zeus doesn't exist, and therefore there is no God, is as logical as saying, "Bugs Bunny doesn't exist, therefore there are no rabbits." One does not necessitate or invalidate the other.

"I don't like the God of the Bible." I find this argument pervasive, although not persuasive. It is in our discussions. It is on the internet. It is even in many of the books on atheism and agnosticism. This is also a complicated argument because it assumes one understands the God of the Bible. Many who use this as a reason for unbelief haven't spent a great deal of time digging into the true nature of the biblical God. They are satisfied to read a story, typically from the Old Testament, and say, "Nope, I won't have anything to do with a God that destroyed . . ."

In a trial, if this argument were on the witness stand, I would cross-examine it in two ways. First, I would probe how well the person knew the biblical God. So much of what is said about him is out of context. That doesn't mean it isn't true, but historical truth exists in historical contexts. The Bible is a collection of stories and events that happened over thousands of years in various historical epochs and cultures that render some of those stories not so easily read and understood, especially the oldest ones.

Failure to put a story into context can radically alter one's perception. It is like saying, "It was a beautiful day . . ." and failing to read the rest of the account: ". . . until the tornado hit!" Or claiming to represent Charles Dickens *A Tale of Two Cities* by saying only, "It was the best of times."

A second line of cross-examination centers on the plain fact that this complaint really isn't a proof God doesn't exist. From a cold perspective, what does it matter if one "likes" God as to whether he exists? The cynic might even ask, "Do you think he likes you?"

There are a few people I don't like, but they still exist. There is a lot of food I don't like, but it still exists. If someone says, "I don't like the God of the Old Testament! He is a misogynist, sadistic, murdering, infanticide-promoting God!" Then whether God *is* such a God is worthy of examination. But whether God is "that kind of God" or whether he isn't, that is not proof he does or doesn't exist.

Please understand, I am not suggesting that God isn't worthy of our "liking." He is worthy of our love, respect, praise, and adoration. I would suggest that those who genuinely think of God in negative ways spend a bit of time reading of Jesus in the Gospel of John, a place where they would see God on display.

"The Bible seems wrong and error-ridden." I must say this argument is both naive and without logic. The naiveté stems from a lack of understanding of what the Bible is, at least in its own claim. The Bible contains narrative, poetry, proverbial wisdom, law, prophetic visions, and more. Each genre of literature found in the Bible proceeded from a culture and a language quite different from today. That means that not only must the language be translated, something done quite well but with inherent limitations, but also the culture must be translated. That is much more difficult.

People who read the Bible only through a twenty-first-century Western lens do not do justice to the richness found in original writings. This limited read also gives one a false impression of what the Bible says, allowing one to find "contradictions" and "errors." In the last section of this book, I examine the creation story in the Bible and compare it to modern science. This exemplifies how the Bible can be misread by the modern mind, concluding that the Bible contradicts science, when in a proper reading, it doesn't.

"Religion has done bad things." This is an indictment against the practices of people, not proof there is no God. To try and use this as proof there is no God would have the logical equivalent that if I could show religion has done good things then there must be a God. As handy as that might be, especially to people who knew the works of Mother Teresa, it simply isn't logical proof. Similarly, if one can show that atheism has "done bad things," would that be regarded as proof there is no atheism?

A fair extension of this argument is, "Well, religion not only does bad things, but God doesn't seem to stop his people from that!" In other words, if there was a God, would he let such stuff go on in his name? This extended argument I will deal with later, but I acknowledge it for the reader here.

History is replete with examples of both great deeds of compassion done in the name of God as well as horrific deeds of hatred. But the key isn't so much what happens in the name of religion as to what role God might play in those events. Hence, I deal with these things later in sections where I look at the philosophical underpinnings that call forth goodness from biblical teaching, as well as potential destruction that comes from atheism. For now, however, it is fair enough to know simply that what religion does or doesn't do, is not in itself a reflection of whether there is a God.

"If God did exist, nothing would be wrong with the world or people." This one always surprises me. It is a classic "straw man" argument. Labeling a straw man argument goes back at least to 1520 when Martin Luther defended himself against attacks on his views about the Eucharist. Luther pointed out that his critics were themselves making the assertions which they then criticized. The assertions weren't Luther's: "They assert the very things they assail, or they set up a man of straw whom they may attack."[14]

The person basing his or her atheism on this argument bases their unbelief on what he or she thinks God should be, and then finds that such a God doesn't exist.

This argument doesn't deal with whether there might be a God who allows people to make choices. Not all gods would stop people from being people. Is God supposed to be one who stops alcohol from affecting the driver who has had it in excess? Is God supposed to make it a magical world where the laws of nature bend willy-nilly to ensure that someone who falls doesn't hit the ground? Is God supposed to make humans into machines where they have no free will but simply perform as programmed? Is God to run the world as a well-disciplined kindergarten class?

These are views that do not mean there is no God. They simply mean "I don't think the kind of God I would like exists." That certainly isn't a proof that no God exists.

As an aside, in the second century, a fellow named Marcion (c. 85–c. 160) believed there were multiple gods, including a god of the Old Testament and a god of the New Testament. Marcion would say that of the Old Testament god, "He is a mean sort of fellow!" Of course, it would never do to answer Marcion and say, "I can prove there is no God, because if God existed, there would be nothing wrong with the world." Marcion would say, "Oh, you must be arguing that there is not a *good god*, not that there is *no god*!"[15]

While I don't agree with Marcion that there are multiple gods, his approach does point out the logical flaw of saying, "If I were God, the world would be different; therefore God must not exist."

"Try praying, and watch it fail." Trying to prove or disprove the existence of God by what one experienced from prayer is always somewhat iffy. Some say prayer hasn't worked, and I have seen cases that might prompt such a view. My wife's brother had a brain tumor that we prayed God would heal. Pray as we might, however, Alan died. Does this mean there is no God? Or does it mean that God accounted for this? Or does it mean that God lets the world go by on its own? There are lots of answers before one says, "This means there is no God."

Similarly, when one of our daughters got the sonogram results of an incurable, clearly seen birth defect in one of the twins she was carrying, she called us in tears to pray about it. Then a week or so later, she went in for more testing, and the sonogram "miraculously" showed the birth defect gone. Does this mean God must exist? To us, it was certainly an answer to prayer. But I am not sure that will convince others, even if they see the sonogram pictures.

One might think to search the scientific literature for peer-reviewed studies of whether prayer is effective. Even that is fraught with difficulties, however. Consider one study published in the *Journal of Reproductive Medicine* in 2001.[16] That study, conducted by K. Y. Cha and D. P Wirth, was a prospective, double-blind, randomized clinical trial in which patients and providers were not informed about the intervention. The design is considered the gold standard for evidence-based medicine. The setting was an in vitro–fertilization program at Cha Hospital, Seoul, Korea. The patients were 219 women aged 26-46 years who were consecutively treated with IVF-ET ("in vitro fertilization-embryo transfer") over a four-month period. Prayer groups in the United States, Canada, and Australia carried out intercessory prayer for one group of random women. The statisticians and investigators were masked from which women were prayed for and which were not until all the data had been collected and clinical outcomes were known.

This removed any placebo effect. The clinical pregnancy rates in the two groups were the main outcome measure. The Cha study showed a statistically significant outcome in both pregnancy rates and implantation rates.

Some studies have found similar results to the Cha study, while other studies have failed to show a statistically significant outcome from prayer. In 2000, a year before Cha's study was published, J. A. Astin and others completed and published a review of studies with the following features: random assignment, placebo or other adequate control, publication in peer-reviewed journals, clinical (rather than experimental) investigations, and use of human participants. Astin's study was published in a top-flight journal, *The Annals of Internal Medicine*.[17]

Astin studied twenty-three different trials that met the criteria. Of the twenty-three studies, thirteen (57 percent) yielded statistically significant treatment effects, nine showed no statistically significant effect over control interventions, and one showed a negative effect. So, does one now accept the reality of God? Does one first break down the studies into who was doing the intercessory prayer or into which faith the prayers were offered?

I have a doctor who is a dear friend of almost twenty years. He is an avowed atheist. But he has told me whenever I or someone I care for is sick, he believes in prayer. He can't explain it, but he says most of the good scientific literature supports the power of prayer in healing.

Prayer is a lot more complicated than simply being a litmus test for God's existence. This scenario of answered/unanswered prayers contains many more possibilities and explanations. One can't use this to prove there is no God.

"Experiment by asking Jesus to appear." This argument assumes Jesus is a genie in a bottle obligated to come and dance when we ask him to. This is not an argument, but arrogance. I exist. I get asked to make appearances often. I frequently say no.

That said, many will tell you that they have seen Jesus. They see him in the lives of people he has changed. He is not a physical person on earth anymore, but he is present in the hearts and minds of his followers. The apostle Paul explained the presence of Jesus being in Spirit when he wrote to the churches in southern Turkey, a letter called Galatians. "And because you are sons, God has sent the Spirit of his Son into our hearts, crying, 'Abba! Father!'" (Gal 4:6). People who make assertions based on asking Jesus to appear aren't really making logical arguments that there is no biblical God.

To some, these arguments may seem silly. Yet they are trumpeted over and over. Many who espouse these arguments are speaking from a position that is meaningful to them. One lawyer with whom I was discussing these things was earnest in his concerns. I walked through the logic of his concerns, and he was a bit shocked to see that they were less substantive than he realized.

With the idea of "praying and seeing if anything happens," I wondered what the lawyer was "praying" that was failing. His prayer was something like, "God, if you are there, lift up this rock and move it from here to there." I suggested that putting God to that kind of test isn't really prayer, nor is it really the role of people to make such demands. I then walked through the biblical ideas of God putting people on earth to make the earth a better place, to show God's love and caring for others, and to do all of this to reflect the goodness of God in a dark world often devoid of caring. I explained that God informs his people that if we seek his help in those things, he is faithful to help us. That help can be giving us insight, opportunity, resources, strength, and more to accomplish his will. I then urged my friend to try praying more like this,

> God, I'm not sure you're there. I don't know how to pray. But if you are there, I believe you want me to help those in need, to have compassion on those hurting, and to show love for others. Help me to understand and to be that person I should be. Help my unbelief. Show me your love for me and teach me to show that love to others.

I told my friend if he was sincere in his search, that he would find God answers that prayer powerfully and profoundly.

Over time, this friend moved from unbelief to faith, but the move wasn't simply from dissembling his intellectual obstacles to faith. It was also from a compassionate and patient consideration of his objections.

That said, many intellectual atheists like Dawkins and Harris would likely shunt aside a number of these arguments saying, "Don't ascribe those to me! Those are arguments of atheists who are not so carefully thinking things through." They might accuse me of constructing a straw man, akin to what I have already brought into this conversation. I don't dismiss that reply of Dawkins and others.[18] But I do note that real people express these real concerns, and they are worthy of one's time to consider fairly.

I find that these atheists frequently grab beliefs of some Christians or others who are less thoughtful and use those as the "beliefs" that they then dissemble, mock, or even destroy. I read what Dawkins, Harris, and others say, "religious people" believe, and I quickly recoil and say, "Not me!" I include these lesser arguments trying to prove there is no God both because they are still out in prominent places, and because this shows that on both sides of the debate or proof scales, we must not accept that the painted views of others are accurate and full.

When all is said and done, I cannot find any real argument of substance that proves there is no God. I can find arguments that shift the burden onto those who believe there is a God, premised on the idea that a default position should be "no God." Of course, since this default position cannot be justified, it is really just a position taken with a blind acceptance.

The reader may be asking, "Where is your proof, Mark?" Or "What goes on the 'belief' side of the scales?" That proof for me comes in my discussion of agnosticism in the next chapters.

In his book *The End of Faith*, Sam Harris makes the point that religions are intolerant, and this is indicative of a problem in believing in God. Each religion will not tolerate the possibility that another religion is right, hence they all have some exclusivity claim. Harris believes this to be a reason for thinking religions are all false. In fact, there is a bit of intellectual hypocrisy going on.

Around 90 percent of the world claims subscription to some religion that has an understanding there is a God. That leaves ten percent not believing in God in any way, shape, form, or fashion. The 90 percent might debate over what that God is or isn't, what he or she should be called, and whether he or she is one or many. But they agree there is something beyond humanity we call God (or gods). It is the atheist who has the intolerant view that all 90 percent of the world is wrong, that no one in any religion has it right, that only the few atheist elites have figured out the truth that there is no God.

Ultimately, I find the atheist's position is taken without evidence and just shifts the burden of proof.

5

AGNOSTICISM, EVIDENCE, AND THE BIG QUESTIONS

I WAS TRYING A BENZENE CASE. Over four hundred families were living in a subdivision with the community water well pumping into their homes water polluted with over ten thousand times the legal level of benzene. Benzene is a clear hydrocarbon that is poisonous. It causes serious illnesses, including certain types of leukemia. It does *not* belong in drinking water.

The court carved out five families for the first trial, including a twelve-year-old boy who had spent the last two years battling for his life with leukemia. All these families had used the water as their principal source of cooking, drinking, and bathing for years.

The benzene came from an underground blowout of a high-pressure oil and gas well from fifty years before. The blowout leaked the equivalent of eleven NFL football stadiums of benzene into the aquifer used by the subdivision. The oil company failed to report the blowout and never pulled out the leaked hydrocarbons.

A key issue I had to prove was that the benzene caused the medical problems the plaintiffs suffered. In the American system, the plaintiffs go first. If the plaintiffs put forward an adequate case of proof, the

defendants then present their case, offering any contrary evidence. I
had reached the point where the defense was putting on its case.

The defendant's lawyer called to the stand a toxicologist who supposedly was an expert in what is toxic to people. The fellow testified that
ten thousand times the legally acceptable level of benzene in drinking
water was absolutely safe. The expert told the jury that since even that
high level of benzene was safe, there was no way the benzene at issue had
caused the plaintiffs' medical conditions. Court recessed for the night,
and I was set to begin cross-examining the witness the next morning.

After court, I returned to my office. I met with a chemist from Rice
University, and I asked him to prepare me a mason jar of water con-
taminated with benzene at ten thousand times the legal level. He did
so, sealing the jar and marking it appropriately with the benzene level.
I took it with me to court the next morning.

After the jury entered and sat down, the judge told me to begin my
cross-examination. I started by pointing out the large sums of money
the oil company paid the witness in return for his testimony. Once that
was established, I leaned in toward the witness and spoke in a private
tone, as if my question and his answer would be just between him and
me, even though everyone in court could clearly hear us. I said, "You
don't really believe that stuff you said yesterday about this level of
benzene being safe, do you?" My "do you?" was not as if I might wonder
what his answer was. I spoke it as a statement, as if, "You and I know
you didn't believe any of that, you were just paid to say it, so you said it."

The witness was still playing his part as a hired gun, so he said, "Yes,
I meant every word of it!" I played out the moment a bit longer and said,
"Come on; you and I both know you are saying it because they paid you
to, but you don't *really* believe it. Right?" He disagreed again, exclaiming, "Of course I believe it."

At that point I pulled out my jar of water with benzene at the full ten
thousand times the legal limit at issue in our case. I showed it to him,
showed the certificate of contents, showed it was sealed by the chemist,
and then I asked the real question. I said, "Sir, if you *really* believe what

you are saying, then I am sure you will have no problem drinking this jar of benzene-contaminated water in front of the jury right now."

The witness was stunned. He didn't see it coming. The lawyers for the oil company were also stunned. They wanted to object, but they knew that the jury would see through such efforts. The witness sat uncomfortably, and everyone could see him shuffling in the witness seat. (This witness should never be a poker player, because he wore his thoughts plainly on his face.) You could see as he sat there that he was thinking, *If I drink this, we will likely win the case. Of course, I may get horribly sick from it because it clearly isn't safe.*

Then as the silence in the courtroom mounted with me holding the jar in front of him, everyone could read his continued thoughts, *Of course, if I don't drink it, we may lose the case . . . but then I will be safe. . . . And they pay me whether we win or not.* Then it occurred to him he might be able to bluff me, and that would be the best way out. So he leaned forward and started to reach out toward the jar. His bluff was obvious. I could see the panic underlying his movement, and I had no hesitancy walking forward and thrusting the jar to him. Realizing his bluff was called, he leaned back in his chair and pulled his hand away. He meekly offered, "I'm not going to drink it. The chemist may have gotten the proportions wrong!"

The jury, the judge, and everyone in the courtroom could immediately tell the truth. That man might be testifying that the water was safe, but when pressed into whether he would put his life on the line, he wouldn't. His actions did not match what he claimed to believe.

There is something about one's actions that betrays truth. A person may say one thing or another, but one's actions show what is real. People may truly believe one thing or another, but their actions will still betray reality. Many people may not want to see it or admit it, but reality isn't dependent on what people see or admit. I may believe gravity has no effect on me, but when you see me standing, you will see it does. I live in a world of gravity, whether I believe it or not. My life shows reality despite what I believe. Reality is real.

This focus on reality is my cross-examination theme on the agnostic philosophy and belief system: the need for consistency between who people are and what they do. I need consistency between *who I am, what I see, and how I live.* I can't find that in agnosticism.

As I use the term, agnostics are undecided about God. When they weigh the evidence in favor of God against the evidence that there is no God these people fall into the camp that there is insufficient evidence to establish one or the other. I believe their consideration of the proof is blinded to critical evidence, however.

Agnosticism, if thoughtful, must admit one of two possibilities: there is a God, or there isn't. If there is a Divine One (or more), certainly another level of examination centers on the type and significance of God. But if there is no God, then the discussion is over. Atheism reigns. Here is the rub: agnosticism can sound like an homage to intellectual humility. It sounds thoughtfully humble to say, "I just don't know." Yet at its core this humility often masks other motives. Some fear examining the issues. Some likely just don't care. Yet all should care. All should be motivated. Because one of two situations must be true. Either there is a God or there isn't, and both answers have profound ramifications on how one lives her or his life.

So I examine the evidence. I look to see not only ideas and arguments, but I examine reality to see what is true. I want to see if reality comports with one side of the scales or the other. Do people live in ways that align with a view of reality that there is no God? I find it doesn't. Like the expert in the benzene case, people handily say one thing, but their lives evidence another.

While I have yet to find an agnostic whose life aligns with his or her view that there is no God, I do find the opposite to be true. I find the lives even of unbelievers to be consistent with the existence of God. If everyone's life is consistent with the existence of God, I find it difficult to embrace the idea (there is no God) that is contrary to what everyone sees and lives.

I model this for myself by turning a legal pad the long way and then setting down on one side of the legal pad what reality is in a world with no God, while setting on the other side what reality is in a world where

God exists. Those two competing worldviews leave a drastically different reality of what life should be like, of what you and I should care about, and of how society should function.

Consider the legal pad looking like this:

COMPETING VIEWS OF REALITY AND THE WORLD

1. Humans are sacks of chemicals, random remnants of cosmic stardust.

2. Parts of "human" chemical sacks have electrical interactions called *thoughts*.

3. The electrical interactions in "human" chemical sacks differ from the electric interactions in other animals.

Deductions: There is nothing that exists that objectively sets "right" and "wrong." Nothing in the universe dictates that some chemical/electrical interactions are inherently "evil." *Good, bad,* etc. are labels that stem from electric interactions (thoughts) but are not based on anything beyond the ingrained electrical impulses of the "human" chemical sacks.

Implications: Some chemical sacks have electrical interactions that make them "think" they are of more cosmic importance than another, but space dust is space dust.

1. Outside of the universe is an infinite, personal, and moral "God" or Being responsible for the universe's existence.

2. Humans are unique among living beings because people bear an imprint (image) of God, by being both moral and personal.

3. Humans exist to be in a personal relationship with God.

4. Humans do not measure up fully to God's morality, making a truly harmonious relationship impossible by itself.

5. Only God can provide a just mechanism to establish that personal relationship, all while maintaining and not compromising God's just and moral character.

Deductions: "Right" and "wrong" have meaning, whether people accept it or not. They are defined by and rooted in the morality of God.

Implications: People are not mere space dust. People have dignity and honor as beings bearing the image of God.

Figure 5.1. This illustrates some of the possibilities of reality when comparing the world with no God to the world with God

Figure 5.1 helps to illustrate some of the possibilities of reality vis-à-vis comparing the world with no God to the world with God. If there is no God, then reality is described on the left. This would be where all humanity lives, and whether anyone acknowledges it or not, the logical deductions from that worldview must be reality.

If, however, the Judeo/Christian worldview is correct, then reality is described on the right (assuming I have accurately annotated the basics of the Judeo/Christian worldview). That means everyone is living in the reality of the views on the right, even if they believe the views on the left. Even the one who believes there is no God lives in the reality of views on the right. This is the benzene case. Their lives, if the worldview on the right is correct, are not lived in harmony with their worldview on the left. Reality betrays the truth.

It is like people who have the flu but refuse to admit it. They say they are fine, but they shiver from a high fever and have aches, a runny nose, and more. The words "I am not sick" are betrayed by the reality of life. They might really believe they are fine, but the evidence indicates the truth.

So one immediate way to test the two competing worldviews is the benzene test. Who will live a life consistent with their worldview? If people live consistent with the view on the right, even when they intellectually try to assert the left view as correct, their actions betray the truth. I can see reality evidenced by how people live.

This is key as I examine the evidence for God and weigh it against the evidence there is no God. When I do, I come down on the side that there is a God.

Weighing different worldviews against reality may not seem like evidence to some people. Some might accept it as evidence, but they think it soft evidence at best. Is it fair to consider what people experience and see how well it aligns with the ideas of reality? Of course it is!

Consider again the different types of evidence for different things I want to prove or disprove. One type of evidence is the scientific method. This is where one forms a hypothesis, develops testable predictions ("If this, then that . . ."), tests the predictions, gathers data, and sets that data against the hypothesis for analysis.

Returning to the benzene case, one of the things I needed to prove is that benzene can cause the type of leukemia the young man had. There are studies that utilize the scientific method, albeit in a slightly altered form, that are based in epidemiology. This means that groups of those exposed to benzene in excessive amounts are compared to groups that have only background levels of exposure (those levels people are exposed to in modern life—pumping gasoline, etc.). Through statistics, scientists are able to prove to a 95 percent certainty that benzene indeed is associated with an increase in certain leukemia types. (It gets complicated, but "Bradford Hill factors" are then used to establish whether the association might arise to causation.[1])

The scientific method works for certain areas of science, but it has limitations, much like a ruler works for measuring some things but not others. Many scientists operate with the scientific method, and they try to use that method with issues of faith. This stems from one of the strengths and weaknesses of the modern world and its education system—the need for specialization. There is a saying, "To a person whose only tool is a hammer, every problem looks like a nail." Because people tend to use the tools they have, when someone spends their academic training learning the scientific method as the reliable testing method for determining truth, they have an inadequate toolbox for measuring truth outside the realm of natural science. The tendency is naturally for these scientists to use that method.

But the scientific method does not work for proving truth in several arenas. One of the things I had to "prove" in the benzene case was that the oil company was malicious and intentional in its actions. No one can prove motives of the heart, malice, or intent with the scientific method. Relatedly, I had to prove whether the young boy suffered mental anguish from the leukemia experience. If so, how much anguish? I can't measure mental anguish with the scientific method, yet I still had to prove those things.

Consider the questions jurors are asked to determine if the death penalty is appropriate. For the death penalty to be imposed in Texas, for example, the jury must find proof on three different questions:

- Is there a probability that in the future the defendant would commit criminal acts of violence that would constitute a continuing threat to society?

- In a capital murder case, did the defendant in taking the life of the deceased, intend to kill the deceased, or anticipate that a human life would be taken?

Only if there is a unanimous answer of yes to both above questions does the third question get asked:

- Taking into consideration all the evidence and circumstances, the defendant's character and background, and the personal moral culpability of the defendant, are there sufficient mitigating circumstances to warrant that a sentence of life in prison without parole be imposed, rather than a death sentence?

While many people recoil at the death penalty, the rightness or wrongness of capital punishment is not the point here. My point is that everything necessary to "prove" the elements of the death penalty, an ultimate decision on life and death, is not subject to the scientific method. Moral culpability can't be measured by a ruler. No lab test can determine if mitigating circumstances are sufficient to warrant parole.

Does that mean there is no evidence on these issues? Of course not! There is solid evidence on which one can base a verdict. There is evidence that is adequate to "prove" the elements of these cases.

Science works for science. The existence of God is not a science. You don't use the tools of nature to prove something that is not a part of nature. If anyone is thinking she or he does not believe in God because there is no scientific proof of him, that person has wrongly limited the field of inquiry and ignores massive amounts of evidence.

Whether one realizes it or not, everyone lives in a broader world of proof than a laboratory. I bring this broader toolbox of proof to the cross-examination of agnosticism and I walk away seeing the evidence for God as greater than the evidence against God.

My evidence is formulated from my life and that of others. There are core questions I need answered to make sense of who I am and who others are. In thinking about these questions, I analyze them as I did the drinking of the benzene water. I am looking for answers that are consistent with life.

THE BIG QUESTIONS

Certain questions in life arise from the realities of my life, from things I experience, and from things I value. These same questions arise when I look at the lives of others, whether they are people of faith or not. These questions frame the reality testing. One rightly asks, "Under which worldview do these questions find adequate answers?" My examination of whether God exists depends on my analysis of these questions.

Is there objective right and wrong, and if so, why? By *objective* I mean something that exists totally apart from perception. In other words, it doesn't matter how one person or another, one culture or another, feels about a matter. It simply is, whether anyone realizes it or not. In this sense, *objective* is the opposite of *subjective*. Something is subjective if it arises from one's own thoughts. Something is objective if it already existed and one's thoughts discover it, as opposed to creating it.

Consider an example. For subjective morality, I suggest how one prioritizes spending money. Is it right to spend $75,000 on a certain car when $65,000 would buy a different, still tremendous car, leaving $10,000 to help those in need? These decisions are subjective. The answer could rightly vary from person to person. But among the morality that is objectively right or wrong, most will admit that rape is wrong, regardless of whether the rapist thinks it is or not. Similarly, no one I've met truly defends the actions of Hitler and the Third Reich as a valid moral choice.

Most admit, either verbally or by their lives, that there is something that truly is called "right," and something truly called "wrong," whether I like it or not. It is hardwired into human bodies that some things are wrong, regardless of how I or others may feel about them. Hence, most people will agree that sexual assault of a child, simply because someone wants it, is wrong. Anyone who commits such behavior is considered morally degenerate, that is, not normal.

The key question is what makes "wrong" wrong? There must be some reason why these things are self-evidently wrong, and this question needs answering. Then, importantly, one's intellectual understanding needs to align with the way one lives.

Why is there beauty? Compare a view from a prison cell, with four walls of grey cinder blocks, to a view of snow-capped Rocky Mountains, with the aspen trees flocked on the sides reflecting light in shimmers. I have heard many people exclaim about the Rocky Mountains, "That is *beautiful!*" I have never heard anyone say that of the grey cinder block cell. What is it about people that there is this concept of "pretty"? I'm pretty sure (pun intended) my dog doesn't have it. Is it simply a more developed brain that finds different views having a different chemical effect on our brains? Maybe, but even that calls out the question, Why? Is beauty objective, subjective, or both?

What makes justice and fairness important? I know many people who don't like certain ideas of "God." One that is constantly repeated in different forms is, "If there is a God, why do bad things happen to good people? Why do evil people prosper? If there is a God, at least if he or she is a good God, then these things wouldn't happen!" These are good questions worthy of attention, but first, look at what is inherent in the questions.

There is an underlying premise that everyone has. It is that justice and fairness are attributes one expects in someone that is good. People bristle at injustice. No one likes to be treated unfairly. This raises the big questions for examination: Why is that? What is there about people that seems hardwired for justice and fairness? Which worldview offers an explanation that is consistent with the way people live?

Is there any basis for human dignity and honor? Most every parent has had the opportunity to say to their children, "I am proud of you!"

There are things that people do that are admirable. I admire the soldiers who give their lives for their country and loved ones. I admire the first responders who place their lives on the line to protect and serve the communities where they live. I watch some people respond to the highs and lows of life, and sometimes I wince while at other times I pause in respect and appreciation.

Are honor and dignity real or hollow concepts masquerading as truth? Is there really such a thing as being rightfully proud of what someone else does? Can I rightly say that some people have dignity and honor? What do I model in life and what would my worldview predict?

Why do people uniquely value humanity? Related to the previous question, what is it about people that sets them apart from other collections of atoms? Why do I value humanity in ways I don't value other plants, insects, and animals? Who is willing to eat deceased people or use them as animal feed? Most people will eat other animals, or at least swat the nuisance mosquito. But people don't so quickly extinguish human life. Why are humans set apart from other animals? Is it because there is some objective value to being able to plan? To talk? To laugh? To contemplate death? Do people simply draw lines at some point as to which layer of conscious life is more worthy of equal treatment than others? Do people live consistently with their worldview on this?

Why do people seek meaning and significance in life? Most everyone lives with the recognition that there must be more to life than simply eating, breathing, and eventually dying. People try to find value and meaning in work, in relationships, in leisure time, and even in death. Why is that? What is it that says, "There must be more to life"? Why do people pursue and, to some measure, find meaning? Why do people despair if they are unable to find meaning? Why does "meaning" mean anything? What does each worldview model predict and what do people's lives demonstrate?

Why do I do things I don't really want to do? Why do I fail to measure up to even my meager goals and plans? Why can't I simply make up my mind to diet and do it? Why, if I decide to exercise daily, do I quit before reaching my goals? Why do I find it hard to forgive others who have wronged me? Why do I dislike people I want to like? Why do I do things I have decided not to do and fail to do things I have decided to do? Many, if not most, of these things are good for me, yet I am unable to achieve them! Has evolution just turned me into someone who is incompetent at things that are very important? Have people evolved into things that have a self-destruct button? Which worldview model more closely aligns with how people live in this regard?

These questions demand answers that align with one's view of reality. Why are these things so? What kind of worldview explains these things? How can one construct a view of people and the natural world where these things make sense?

The answers to these questions, and in some cases simply having the questions, drive me to conclude there is a God. These questions are not the only ones that demand an answer congruent with one's view of reality. There are negative perceptions that weigh against the idea that reality includes an all-powerful and all-loving God. These big questions also need addressing.

Why is there suffering? Suffering is real. It can happen on unimaginable scales. The Holocaust, cancer in children, starvation, and more all demand an answer for why there is suffering, especially if one believes in an almighty and loving God.

If God is real, then why can't people see him? As a simplistic charge, I considered it earlier, but beyond that consideration it merits additional analysis. One must ask why God doesn't show himself to remove all doubt if God is truly there.

If God is real, why are so many prayers unanswered? When prayers are answered, one might wonder if the prayer made a difference. But when prayers are unanswered, people seem to know the prayers made no difference at all. Why is that? If there is a God who wants to hear my prayers, and who promises to be responsive, why do some prayers, some *very good* prayers for *very good* things, go unanswered?

How does God mesh with science and the reality of the cosmos?
One thing I am relatively sure of is what I experience and know from life. I know water is H_2O and that it can freeze at 32° F (0° C). I know the moon is not Swiss cheese, and I know that dinosaurs once roamed the earth. How do I mesh science with views of a God, especially the Judeo-Christian God? How does this mesh considering a Bible that seems to defy the scientific theory of evolution?

Each of these questions also demands rigorous analysis. A real view of the world, a valid understanding of reality, must fit snugly with all the evidence I have at my disposal. If people understand the world to be only A, B, and C, then that is good if the evidence is all A, B, and C. But if I think the world is only A, B, and C, and the evidence is A, B, and D, then I have a problem. Either I have not properly assessed our evidence, or I need to shift my worldview.

I analyze all these pieces of evidence to see if there is a worldview that consistently explains the totality of evidence. I think it best to think of weighing evidence again using the picture of balancing scales, like one sees Lady Justice holding in many courts around America.

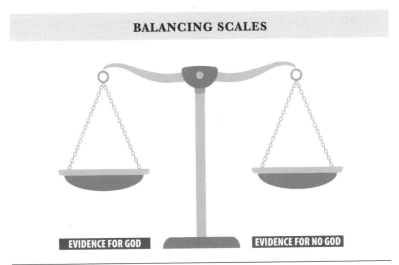

BALANCING SCALES

EVIDENCE FOR GOD   EVIDENCE FOR NO GOD

Figure 5.2. By putting all of the evidence for God on one side and all of the evidence against God on the other, one can make a constructive proof based on the available evidence: God or no God

I want to read other thoughtful writers on both sides of this debate, process their thoughts, think on my own about the issues, and then line up the evidence on both sides of the scales. Then I can assess which side outweighs the other.

Aligning up evidence *against* God, the most prominent and most often cited are the problem of suffering, God's invisibility, unanswered prayer, and natural explanations for nature and the wonders of the universe.

Aligning up evidence *for* God includes considering the seven questions set forward earlier and measuring them to the models of belief and behavior people exhibit (as well, perhaps, as some fundamental natural questions not fully answered by current knowledge of science).

One of the things that I have learned over decades of trial work, sorting through evidence on both sides of the scales, is this: It is not always as simple as one set of evidence outweighing the other. The whole truth includes all evidence. So, as I examine the evidence against God, I need to see if the idea of God's existence provides any answers to the evidence against that existence. What I should see is that a worldview model makes sense of *all* the evidence, and not merely part of it.

In other words, are there legitimate explanations of suffering, God's invisibility, unanswered prayer, and the natural explanations of the world's order that align with the existence of God? Similarly, are there legitimate explanations for the seven questions, in a world in which there is no God?

Everyone can work through this to a conclusion. One does not need a degree in philosophy, science, or law. Simply look carefully at the evidence for and against, examine it for logical consistency, consider the credibility, weigh it against the experiences of life, and determine which truth best fits the evidence. Doing so one can rightly decide whether the existence of God is something that one should affirm or whether one is properly left saying, "I can't reach a conclusion" (agnosticism).

Figure 5.3 is the set of evidence to consider and place into the scales.

WEIGHING THE EVIDENCE

EVIDENCE FOR GOD

EVIDENCE OF NO GOD

EVIDENCE TO BE CONSIDERED:

- Is there objective right and wrong? If so, why?
- Why is there beauty?
- Why are justice and fairness important?
- Is there any basis for human dignity and honor?
- Why do people uniquely value humanity?
- Why do people seek meaning and significance in life?

- Why do my actions fail to meet my standards?
- Why is there suffering?
- Why can't I see God?
- Why do so many prayers seem unanswered?
- How does God mesh with science to make sense of the cosmos?

Figure 5.3. The set of evidence to consider and place into scales

Let me analyze each of these pieces of evidence in the following chapters.

6

MORALITY, BEAUTY, AND JUSTICE

Somewhere each person should have to account for what is real and what is not. In 2003, Oxford philosopher Nick Bostrom published a paper, "Are You Living in a Computer Simulation?"[1] One option for reality posited by Bostrom was that our "reality" is a computer program built by a posthuman civilization running ancestor-simulations that give some level of awareness to the routines being run in the computer to better realize how life would have evolved. Elon Musk brought Bostrom's idea into the public arena in 2016.[2] The idea wears new clothes in the twenty-first century, but the questioning of reality isn't new. Zhuangzi asked in the fourth century BC whether people are butterflies dreaming to be a human or humans who dream of butterflies. What is reality? Am I real because "I think," as Descartes premised?[3]

Many may not care to ask what is real, but I want to know. I want answers to what is going on in this world and in life. Reality must be a fundamental question. The odds are great that if you are reading these pages, you have already decided, like me, that this life is real. I am a real person. I feel and sense real things. I experience a real life.

That means that there are aspects of who I am, of who you are, and of what this life is like that should be subject to rational analysis and logical deduction. I should be able to use common sense to figure out some answers to some basic questions, including the seven I have asked in chapter five.

IS THERE OBJECTIVE RIGHT AND WRONG, AND IF SO, WHY?

This is a very compelling question. One marvelous writer on this subject is Thomas Nagel. (Fair warning of my bias: Nagel is a law professor [emeritus] at NYU, where I serve on a board, as well as a philosopher.) An atheist, Nagel has written extensively on objective and subjective morality and ethics. He struggles to explain and justify an objective morality without a God to give the objective morality a source. In his book *The View from Nowhere*, he writes insightfully, "Objectivity is the central problem of ethics. Not just in theory, but in life."[4]

It is interesting to look at the history of philosophers debating this point. In Greek thought, these discussions famously include Socrates (c. 470–399 BC), with his textbook dialogue with Euthyphro.[5] Ideas on the subject go back much further than that in Judaic thought.

One way to pose the question is: If I believe there are some objective rights and wrongs, where do these come from? By "objective" right or wrong, I am contrasting it to those rights or wrongs that are "subjective." *Objective* means that it is wrong regardless of how anyone feels or thinks about it, such as Hitler seeking to annihilate a race because he thinks the race inferior. If this is objectively wrong, it doesn't matter how you and I might feel about it. It doesn't matter if Hitler had the support of the German people. This is not a "right or wrong" issue determined by the intellectual elite, the powerful, the majority vote of society, or by designated representatives. It is neither personally nor socially subjective. It is wrong. Period.

Now some people may say there is no objective wrong. In fact, a group of people often labeled *skeptics* by philosophers challenge whether even reason or rationale thought exist as something objective. For these people, everything is subjective, not only morality. Truth are reality are simply an internal decision.

An examination of skepticism is worthy of its own book. But for my purposes here, the skeptic and moral subjectivist both fail the benzene test in the start of this chapter. Go back to the Nagel quotation. Objective morality isn't just a problem in theory; it is a problem in living. That is, does anyone live consistent with the view that there is no objective wrong, and that each person gets to decide what is right and what is wrong? Would these people not get upset if I steal their computer? After all, there is nothing wrong with that if I don't think it wrong. For that matter, is it fair to sexually assault someone just because "it feels right," regardless of how the victim feels about it? Of course not! No one will live that way.

Deep in the human core, people know raping a child is wrong. People know murder is wrong. People know there are some things that are wrong in and of themselves. So where does this wrong come from? Some will say it is a part of nature. The world is simply built that way. Of course, common sense points out the problems with this answer. First, under the "no God" worldview model, all people are is a sack of chemicals with active electrical pulses creating something called *life* and *consciousness*. Everyone and everything in the entire universe is simply a collection of atoms and subatomic particles. Where, in this grand universe, are the atoms that have accumulated in such a way as to make "objective" morality? It doesn't seem to exist on a molecular level!

Furthermore, the idea that nature contains an inherent objective morality doesn't seem borne out by the world. It certainly doesn't seem to be true in the ocean. I have yet to hear of many sharks who think twice about gulping down their neighbor. The sharks do not have a great reputation for passing up a hurt or injured fish as opposed to killing it and using it for the sharks' own purposes (read: *food*).

Some say that sharks might not have developed this "conscious awareness of right and wrong" that other higher conscious animals have. The idea is that "right and wrong" are ingrained in an evolved subconscious. This again involves quite a gymnastic leap of common sense to me. At what point in the history of this little planet in this out-of-the-way part of the solar system in this far-flung region of the universe, did conscious thought evolve to such an extent that what the day before was "fine" suddenly became "wrong"? Not wrong because someone says so, but truly wrong in an objective sense?

I have had long conversations with a smart, kind, and caring fellow who holds this view. What struck me in our dialogues was his utter inability to prove his explanation. He kept falling back on the principle that two plus two is four. "It just is," he would explain. Or he would say, "We live in a universe where some things are just wrong." I asked him to pinpoint when indiscriminate murder became wrong, for it certainly doesn't apply to the fish in the sea from which we allegedly evolved. So, at what point in his thinking through the evolutionary process did indiscriminate killing become *objectively* wrong? He could never explain.

Similarly, I find him and others with his view unable to answer successfully how he could ever justify one morality over another. He would surely (and rightly) abhor it if someone suggested killing those who were mentally or physically challenged by their DNA (children with Down syndrome, for example). He would *know* that was wrong. Yet he would be hard-pressed to sell his ethic over that of a person suggesting that the world's limited resources should be spent on those who help propel humanity along the ladder of evolution. "Culling the herd" is what a cattleman might call it.

To carefully consider the options on this issue, although it may repulse many, I will use the ethics of rape. Is rape wrong? I think most everyone would answer yes. The follow-up question is then the key: Why? Compare the two options: No God or God.

The "No God" model and worldview provides several choices.

Because most people in society say so. This choice doesn't strike me as right. This isn't personal subjectivism, but it is subjective, nonetheless. This is societal subjectivism. It fails to establish an objective morality.

Hitler was elected by popular vote. He had societal support for his programs. That didn't make his programs moral. If I find myself in a tribal culture where society believes it is okay for a victorious tribe to rape the women and children of a defeated tribe, surely I am not saying rape in that circumstance is good.

"Because those in positions of power say so." Again, this choice doesn't strike me as right. If I were to live in a world where the king was allowed any sexual conquest of his choice, without regard to the wishes of the female or male, I would not suddenly think that the king's rape of anyone was now right and moral.

"Because might makes right." This is another loser in the sense that power has an intoxicating effect that justifies all sorts of things that would otherwise be wrong. Just because a man is strong enough to force rape onto a woman, does that make the rape right? Of course not.

"Because the intellectual elite say so." This is not only a poor explanation for me, but it is a scary one. The idea that a select few are empowered to dictate right and wrong for the rest of the world does not provide a sensible reason that rape would be wrong. If those intellectuals were to change their collective minds tomorrow, would that suddenly make rape okay?

"Because it is ingrained into the fabric of the universe that animals of higher consciousness should honor the sexual choices of the individual." Now this makes sense to one intuitively ("in one's gut"), but where does this make sense from a logic perspective? Consider it this way. If there is no God, no higher being, nothing beyond humanity in terms of authority, then all anyone is, in reality, is a sack of chemicals having chemical and electrical reactions. People have come into existence purely by time and chance. By *existence*, all one could mean is that the stardust that eventually became planet earth sorted itself into locations where the chemical soup produced some chemicals that started evolving into more complicated sacks of chemicals, eventually producing the sack of chemicals that is you and me.[6] But how is there a "morality" or "right and wrong" for a sack of chemicals that has no

meaning, no purpose, no direction, nothing except a brief serendip-
itous existence as a sack that can think or realize what it really is?
That is no basis for an objective right and wrong.

"Because science has taught the difference in good and evil." This
idea is rightly taken to task by atheist John Gray who points out that
the assumption that science will support the liberal values of the
atheists like Sam Harris is simply accepted. There is no explanation
why science should do so. I can't say it better than Gray:

> In fact, all these versions of "scientific ethics" are fraudulent, and
> not only because the sciences they invoke are bogus. Science
> cannot close the gap between facts and values. No matter how
> much it may advance, scientific inquiry cannot tell you which
> ends to pursue or how to resolve conflicts between them. . . . The
> reason Harris passes over these questions is not only a lack of
> knowledge on his part. By cultivating a willed ignorance of the
> history of ideas, he . . . can then pass over the fact that the liberal
> values he claims to profess originated in monotheism.[7]

If these were all the choices, I would be stuck. I might retreat away
from the thought there is objective right and wrong. I might think the
smart thing to do would be to live however I wanted to if I could get
away with it.

Fyodor Mikhailovich Dostoevsky (1821–1881) was a Russian philosopher and novelist who explored human psychology in several well-
known books. In *The Brothers Karamazov*, Dostoevsky explored the
questions related to God and morality. His character Pyotr Aleksan-
drovich explained that without God,

> then nothing would be immoral, all things would be lawful, even
> anthropophagy [cannibalism] . . . for every private . . . who be-
> lieves neither in God nor in his own immortality, the moral law
> of nature must instantly be transformed into the complete op-
> posite of the old, religious law, and that selfish egoism even to

the point of evil-doing must not only be lawful to man but must
even be acknowledged to be necessary.[8]

But there is another choice. It is the choice that involves God and
the other worldview model.

*"Humanity is hardwired for objective morality because 'God' is
a moral being and has made humanity to share in that morality."*
This view means that people inherently know what is right and
wrong. It is inscribed into one's DNA as humans. It is part of what
allows one to live successfully, breed prolifically, and promote civil
society. It "works."

Here there is an idea that a being exists outside of our world order.
This being called "God" has a moral structure to him or her (there is no
need to determine the gender of this "God" for this explanation). This
morality is one that God wove into the fabric of the universe, so people
sense it there as well. It is a morality ingrained into humans in a different way from other animals because humans are hardwired with
God's morality. To borrow a Jewish term, humans are "made in God's
image" (Gen 1:26). This choice makes common sense to me. It helps me
understand why I am so acutely aware of right and wrong. It makes
sense of the way people live. It passes the benzene test.

It belies the argument made by the philosopher Walter Sinnott-
Armstrong who spends a good bit of his writing trying to justify his
belief that an atheist can be moral.[9] Yes, an atheist can be moral, because that atheist is hardwired for morality by God. If the worldview
of God existing is right, I would expect many atheists to believe in and
display morality. I would expect Thomas Nagel and others to write
long probing attempts to justify an objective ethic, even though in the
end it becomes subjective to them.[10] After all, even though they don't
subscribe to that worldview, they still live in that world.

Sinnott-Armstrong's writings on the subject betray his failing the
benzene test. He never spends time explaining what *moral* means
because he can trade on the fact that everyone inherently knows. This

is what it means for it to be hardwired into us. I suggest Sinnott-Armstrong misses the problem. The problem is not "Can an atheist be moral?" The problem is, "What is the intellectual reason *why* the atheist *would* be moral?"

Sinnott-Armstrong will say that morality exists because it tracks with what "harms" people. So, rape is wrong because it harms the victim. Again, though, this is a bit of circular reasoning. To say that something is immoral because it harms another is to say that harming another is immoral. Why is that so? Why can society tell Joseph Stalin that he is being immoral because he is harming hundreds of thousands? What is the basis for saying *harm* equals *immoral*?

Similarly, what about Thomas Malthus (1766–1834)? As an early "economist," Malthus was concerned that excess food production leads to excess population. Malthus believed the long-term result was that population growth would outstrip food production. For Malthus, feeding the impoverished might seem good, but over time, ten people would starve for every life one saved through food. Hence the Malthusian hypothesis would say that feeding the poor is immoral because it works to the long-term harm. Should one then make the moral choice and not feed the poor, letting them starve to death?

For one who believes that God sets a moral standard, these issues are easy. One looks to God as the moral standard, and if harming another is immoral then it is immoral. But if people are sacks of chemicals, these issues are far from easy. Why is it immoral for one sack of chemicals to alter another sack of chemicals in a way that makes the altered sack have different chemical reactions? Sinnott-Armstrong has just altered his morality question, shifting it from "Why is immoral immoral?" to "Why is harm immoral?" What makes it inherently wrong to cause a certain kind of chemical reaction that Sinnott-Armstrong believes is harm. Sinnott-Armstrong has merely shifted the argument from *wrong* or *immoral* to *harm*. Who defines *harm*? What some describe as harm may be beneficial to a being that is developing. It may help them stay alive until they can pass along their genetic material. Many a time a surgeon needs to harm someone to save her or his life. Does that constitute harm or is harm measured by the ultimate result? If the life saved is Adolf Hitler, does it constitute harm to save that life?

Here again the reality of God existing gives more structure to the words being used as well as the concept behind the words. If a God exists, and if that God is moral and made humanity (one can read that as "caused to evolve"—creation versus evolution is a red herring at this point) in such a way that people know that harm is not a good thing, then harm isn't simply a ranking of different chemical reactions among different chemical sacks or containers. It is something that is real and significant. Harm should be avoided, as a general rule. The early political philosophy of John Stuart Mill was premised on the maxim that government's only authoritative basis for exercising power over an individual is to prevent harm to others.

This answer also helps me better understand where Richard Dawkins gets it right, and where he misses the boat as he tries to discuss morality in his landmark book *The Selfish Gene*. Dawkins argues that people behave "altruistically . . . for the good of the genes." He posits that (1) people have a genetic structure that is "ruthlessly selfish"; (2) in special circumstances, that selfish gene can best achieve its selfish goals by being altruistic (sometimes being unselfish is the most selfish thing a gene can do); (3) people feed and protect others who share the same genes; and, therefore, (4) humanity has perpetuated this genetic predisposition toward morality or altruism.

Dawkins is certain that there must be something genetically selfish underlying the ideas of universal love, and the welfare of other people. To think otherwise throws a kink in the godless evolution that Dawkins preaches. He affirms,

> If you look at the way natural selection works, it seems to follow that anything that has evolved by natural selection should be selfish. Therefore we must expect that when we go and look at

the behaviour of baboons, humans, and all other living creatures, we shall find it to be selfish. If we find that our expectation is wrong, if we observe that human behaviour is truly altruistic, then we shall be faced with something puzzling, something that needs explaining.[11]

Dawkins is trying to bootstrap his experience and perception of reality onto his science, without providing for the existence of a deity. It leaves him trying to explain why a race that should be focused only on selfish ends, somehow cares about unselfish matters, even finding it a virtue.

If, however, humanity was made with DNA dictating the development of bodies, with a drive toward being fruitful and multiplying, with a drive toward not only individual success, but community success, and pre-programmed by God with an inherent understanding of the value of moral achievement, then the selfish gene is explained, the altruism is explained, the tension between the two is explained, and Dawkins has a much different book to write!

A real predicament exists for those who do not believe that something outside of humanity has defined morality. These people are at a loss to explain the moral language they can't escape using. A case in point is the prominent atheist Michael Ruse. In *The Guardian*, Ruse wrote an opinion piece titled, "God Is Dead. Long Live Morality."[12] He begins the piece asserting, "God is dead, so why should I be good? The answer is that there are no grounds whatsoever for being good. . . . Morality is flimflam."

Notice what Ruse has done? In legal terminology, I would stand up and say, "Objection, your honor, assumes facts not in evidence." The assumption Ruse has made is that there is meaning behind the word *good*. This sums up the whole issue I have with this vis-à-vis agnosticism or atheism. An atheist or agnostic needs to define *good* without just assuming everyone knows what it means. These people use the word in a way that assumes morality; it doesn't prove it. They are evidencing that they are hardwired to know what good is. Where did that hardwiring come from? If it came from nowhere, then not only is morality "flimflam," but the person advocating that people can still be good, as Ruse does, needs to quit using the word *good*.

Instead, use a non-value word like *ping*. Then, to be consistent, I would say that *ping* means some arbitrary behavior that one or more sack of chemicals has agreed to being ping. Now there is no value here. I am not saying that ping is any better or worse than any other choice. After all there is no "better" or "worse" when actions are stripped from valuation. So, I simply have ping. Now I read Ruse or others who advocate morality without sourcing the morality and I rightly have someone saying, "We can do ping if we want to, regardless of whether there is a God." Yes, we can. But what is the value of doing ping versus pong or something else? It is no longer "objective right or wrong." One can no longer say rape is wrong if rape is just ping.

I am left considering the evidence on objective right and wrong and I find no one effectively lives a life consistent with any view other than the idea that there is a real right and wrong, that people are hardwired to it, and that it is more than a chemical reaction in a sack of chemicals. I put this in the scales on the side that there must be someone or something beyond humanity that has given definition to right and wrong, and that people are hardwired into that definition. This is real evidence for God.

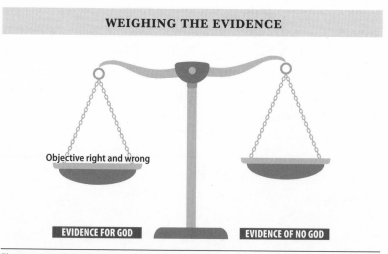

Figure 6.1. Weighing the evidence for the existence of God

WHY IS THERE BEAUTY?

Several notable and thoughtful people who believe in God cite beauty as one of the reasons for belief. Some say that beauty would not predominate in nature, absent a beautiful creator, because the randomness of evolution would produce ugliness. Some use other arguments related to beauty, but I don't go into too much detail on those because these ideas of proof for God all seem to center on the belief that beauty is objective rather than, or in addition to, being subjective. So my efforts at analyzing this piece of evidence center on that question.

If I want to see the "beauty is objective and therefore there is a God" argument, it is well-presented by Augustine (AD 354–430). He is often quoted for his comments about physical beauty being measured against an objective standard.

> Physical beauty . . . can be appreciated only by the mind. This would be impossible, if this "idea" of beauty were not found in the mind in a more perfect form. . . . But even here, if this "idea" of beauty were not subject to change, one person would not be a better judge of sensible beauty than another. . . . This consideration has readily persuaded men of ability and learning . . . that the original "idea" is not to be found in this sphere, where it is shown to be subject to change. . . . And so, they saw that there must be some being in which the original form [of beauty] resides, unchangeable, and therefore incomparable. And they rightly believed that it is there that the origin of things is to be found, in the uncreated, which is the source of all creation.[13]

Some say that the idea of objective beauty is an additional proof for the reality of God and the Judeo-Christian worldview. Because this argument is frequently used by those arguing for the existence of God, I consider the evidence pro and con, weighing it for or against the existence of God. When I do so, I fairly admit that I do not find the evidence persuasive either way. I find it can be consistent with a worldview of a Judeo-Christian God as well as a worldview without God. So, for me, this is not determinative evidence to put on the scales. Instead, it is an example of a piece of evidence that, in fairness, fits multiple models of reality. Consider the evidence and see if you agree with my conclusion.

Many are surprised to learn that the ideas of beauty have been an intense area of study by philosophers throughout history as they consider human nature and the cosmos. What is beauty? How and why does it exist?

There are a few things about beauty that are consistent among the people I've met either directly or through their writings. I know no one who finds beauty in an enclosed grey cinderblock jail cell. People readily proclaim certain things in nature as beautiful. Sunrises and sunsets, blue skies and rainbows, an infant's smile, and the ocean's deep blue are beautiful by most everyone's reckoning. Many human creations also merit the label *beautiful,* including paintings like Da Vinci's *Mona Lisa* or Dali's *Persistence of Memory.* Bach's Toccata in D Minor is a beautiful work of music. People can experience performances of beauty, like the ballet *Swan Lake.* The human body itself can be considered beautiful.

These various examples of beauty may not be to everyone's tastes, but people still see them and designate them as beautiful. And I am drawing a distinction here between *beauty* and *taste.*

Most know the saying that "beauty is in the eye of the beholder," making all beauty subjective. It is conceivable that some might see the grey cinder block cell as beautiful, while others would better find an idyllic scene of nature beautiful. But historically, some argue that regardless of the "eye of the beholder" adage, beauty is not subjective but rather objective. This argument might change the famous adage to "taste, not beauty, is in the eye of the beholder."

The history of debating whether beauty is objective or subjective goes back thousands of years in Western thought. It is one of the most debated questions of philosophical writing on beauty. Among the ancient Greek philosophers, it is a bit difficult to trace the arguments on whether beauty was objective or subjective because the Greek word translated "beauty" (*kalos*—καλός), has a semantic range including "noble" or "admirable." Still, most will concur that a number of prominent Greek philosophers taught that beauty was a "form," something that had an existence outside of people and hence was objective.

Augustine believed in objective beauty and based an argument on that premise. The Greeks would write of beauty as a virtue, including beauty in a person, beauty in relationships like certain shared loves, as well as beauty in artistic creations. The debate was often not whether beauty was objective or subjective, but what made up the form of beauty.

By the time of the philosopher David Hume (1711–1776), philosophy rejected beauty as an objective form, with Hume famously writing, "Beauty is no quality in things themselves: It exists merely in the mind which contemplates them; and each mind perceives a different beauty. One person may even perceive deformity, where another is sensible of beauty; and every individual ought to acquiesce in his own sentiment, without pretending to regulate those of others."[14] From Hume on, most well-known philosophers considered beauty as a subjective reality, not objective.

At some point, this almost breaks down into a semantic argument over what one means *by* "beauty" as opposed to what *is* beauty. Do Hume and others of his persuasion mean *taste* as people use the word in the twenty-first century? Surely taste is subjective. The word itself derives from one of the five senses. I find Bob Dylan's "Tangled Up in Blue" beautiful, but I don't have much appreciation for certain operatic pieces that others might deem beautiful. More likely, these are not questions of beauty, but of taste.

Setting aside questions of taste, some good arguments exist that there is an element of beauty that must be objective, otherwise the word itself has no real meaning beyond a personal attitude of approval. So, for example, I can argue about whether something is beautiful. That seems to denote some aspect of the idea that is objective. Most people all agree on certain things possessing a degree of beauty (for example, a sunset over the ocean, or autumn leaves in New England).

But even this is a bit dicey as an argument, since people may have bred similar tastes as part of natural selection.

I weigh these ideas of beauty being objective, subjective, or a mixture, and it makes a measure of sense to me under either the "God" or "No God" models. With the Judeo-Christian God, I certainly understand both objective and subjective beauty being a reality. God's creation reflects beauty, and the creations of people, who made in God's image can also create, can both see beauty and create beauty. Furthermore, as creatures with independent thoughts, people can easily have differing tastes about what they find beautiful versus what they don't.

If there is no God, then all beauty would necessarily be subjective. *Beauty* becomes synonymous with *taste*. People might view certain things similarly beautiful, but that might be a result of natural selection. For example, if a female peacock picks her mate by the extreme colors and fullness of his tail feather fan, then it might make sense that over time, the successive generations of peafowl will be those who find similar tail feathers beautiful.

On whether beauty is objective or subjective, and on whether it makes more sense under the "God" or "No God" model, I deem it indeterminate. I believe that beauty is real, and I believe it is objective; however, I don't believe the objectivity can be "proven" in the legal sense of "proof." Therefore, as I can find a place for it under either model, for me, the evidence does not weigh in the scales.[15]

WHY ARE JUSTICE AND FAIRNESS IMPORTANT?

Outspoken atheist and entertainer Stephen Fry was interviewed and asked how he might react if after death, he were to come face-to-face with God. Fry, a Cambridge-educated man, replied,

> I'd say, "Bone cancer in children? What's that about? How dare you? How dare you create a world to which there is such misery that is not our fault? It's not right, it's utterly, utterly evil. Why should I respect a capricious, mean-minded, stupid God who

creates a world which is so full of injustice and pain?" That's what I would say.

Fry was then asked if he thought that exchange might secure him entrance into heaven and he replied, "No, but I wouldn't want to. I wouldn't want to get in on his terms. They are wrong."[16]

This is a typical argument raised by many who do not believe in God. The argument is a favorite, I suspect, because it indicts the Judeo-Christian God as unjust and uncaring, while at the same time bolstering the unbeliever as one who is caring.

I believe it proper to ask the hard questions like, "Why bone cancer in children?" It is one I will consider in the next chapter because I believe only the Judeo-Christian explanation for such tragedies makes sense. But at this point, I want to look carefully at feelings like Fry expressed, because by doing so, one can see a strong piece of evidence for the existence of the Judeo-Christian God.

Fry spoke of his refusal to respect a God who creates a world full of "injustice."[17] One must wonder if Fry has given thought to his own statements. Notice that the idea of justice is important to Fry. Ditto for the idea of fairness, as he writes of misery that "is not our fault" or "terms" that are "wrong." Where does that come from? I think it is key evidence for the existence of the Judeo-Christian God.

I would suggest that inherent in humanity is a concept of fairness and justice. Like morality, it appears to be hardwired into the human mind and psyche. Consider how this came to be. Should one believe that people have developed a keen sense of justice and fairness through natural selection? That somehow individuals benefit from fair treatment, and that humanity found it comes only if we ensure fairness to society? Perhaps, but that's a stretch of post hoc analysis.[18] The facts seem to belie such a theory.

In truth, most people don't really want fairness. People want what is best for them, whether it is fair or not. Consider someone born into a nice middle-class family in the United States or somewhere else in

Western civilization. This birthright was not fair, especially when compared to the children born in a starving community in a lesser developed country. Or if I isolate the United States, compare the well-born to someone born to a single mom, diseased by the AIDS virus, strung out on drugs, prostituting herself to get money for her addiction. Comparing that innocent infant to one who is born into common, everyday parents who maintain a job, have a home, car, and hopes for the future, there is no fairness or justice. Yet how do people respond? Generally, "out of sight, out of mind."

Very, *very* few people put the teaching of Jesus into practice and "love their neighbors as themselves." The world doesn't have a society where there is a redistribution of wealth or resources from the heartlands of America to sub-Saharan Africa to aid impoverished children. The United States doesn't have national health care to provide for the needs of infants and children. Everyone will readily admit that health care in the United States, as well as in most countries, is somewhat income dependent. The more money you have, the higher level of health care is accessible.

The observations about fairness extend to justice. People like to say, at least in America, "We believe in justice." Of course, many will trace this prioritizing justice as a trait of the Judeo-Christian heritage of the United States, but set that issue aside.[19] My issue is that while people proclaim the virtues of justice, it isn't an inherent part of practice. A simple look at prison populations shows that "justice" favors the rich majority at the expense of the poorer minority.

Some might want to say that fairness and justice are evolved traits, but the world, historically or currently, doesn't support that. This lack of support is odd when one recognizes that a voice within most everyone cries out that justice and fairness are not only virtues but should be the norm. It comes early in life as children learn to proclaim to an early bedtime, "But that's not fair!" It stays on through life as the Stephen Frys of the world proclaim, "God's not fair!" or, "The injustice of it all!"

It is as hard for people to get away from a sense of the impropriety of injustice and unfairness as it is for objective morality. If there is no real *value* in justice or fairness, then why would Fry even care if God was or wasn't just or fair? Fry could just say, "There is no God, but if he is, then he is" without railing on the issue of, "Then why isn't he *fair?*"

Fry thinks that a good God would run the world like a good kindergarten teacher who fixes when one person takes another's snack, tends to skinned knees, and makes sure Johnny doesn't hit Bobby. For Fry, those concepts are so important that without them, God is not God. Or at least not a good one.

So where do the concepts come from? If there is a Judeo-Christian God, the answer is easy. If there isn't, one is hard-pressed to find a source beyond the fascinating electrical synapses of human sacks of chemicals.

From a Judeo-Christian explanation, we would expect justice and fairness to be hardwired into our beings. Jewish and Christian Scriptures alike teach that people are made in the image of God (Gen 1:26-27). God is also portrayed as a "just" God over and over in Scripture. God even instructed his people to be just, using fair weights and balances, and not cheating others in their transactions (Lev 19:36). Judges were told to be fair to all, regardless of race or income (Deut 1:16).

The prophet Ezekiel took issue with those who challenged the justness of God while holding out themselves as the "judge" of what is just. "Yet the house of Israel says, 'The way of the Lord is not just.' O house of Israel, are my ways not just? Is it not your ways that are not just?" (Ezek 18:29).

It raises the question of why people rail against God for the children with cancer, yet do so without being in the cancer ward, offering solace, help, and more for those who are hurting. God at least offer solace, comfort, and assurance of a better life after death.

With God as a just God, and that God making people in his image, it makes sense that justice is an important concept for people. The issue then becomes, "Why do bad things happen in a world over which God has a measure of control?" That will be considered in more detail when I reach the arguments against God. For now, however, the mere importance of fairness and the affront of injustice denotes to me that somewhere beyond simple chemical sacks of refined stardust, there are ingrained notions of fairness and justice as important standards.

Without God, the notions of fairness and justice really are just semantic terms associated with a cosmic karma.[20] It is as if there must be a moral equivalent of the physical law that "every action has an equal and opposite reaction." But that is not right. Moral laws are not physical laws of inanimate objects. They are from the realm of thoughts and ideas. Without God, those are electro-chemical reactions in the brain. Cosmic karma, without a God-driver to the karma, is really a silly idea. Why would inanimate stardust set up the standard that animated stardust (chemical sacks having certain electric reactions) requires karma?

I find that explanation defying common sense and a stretch. To me, I add the ideas of justice and fairness as important virtues and goals to evidence in favor of a just and fair God as claimed in Judeo-Christian Scriptures.

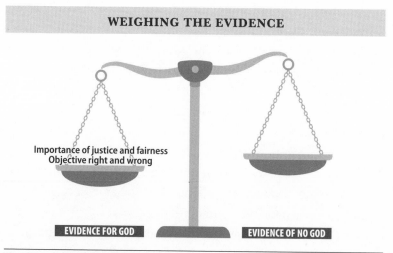

WEIGHING THE EVIDENCE

Importance of justice and fairness
Objective right and wrong

EVIDENCE FOR GOD   EVIDENCE OF NO GOD

Figure 6.2. Adding the ideas of justice and fairness

7

HUMAN DIGNITY AND SIGNIFICANCE

IS THERE ANY BASIS FOR HUMAN DIGNITY AND HONOR?

In 1971, a thin little book titled *Beyond Freedom and Dignity* took the bestseller list by storm. Authored by Harvard behaviorist B. F. Skinner (1904–1990), the book set out a view of humanity that removed the concepts of dignity and honor from rational discussion. Skinner believed that people are sacks of chemicals and no more. For Skinner, the chemicals are first determined by DNA, and then altered by the environment. Those alterations are set by nature's laws, and no one has any real choice in who they are or what they become.

Here is a simplified illustration of Skinner's position. Imagine that I have a jar of vinegar. The chemical makeup of my jar is water (H_2O), acetic acid (CH_3COOH), and likely a few other trace chemicals including flavorings. Next, imagine that I pour into that jar of vinegar a tablespoon of baking soda ($NaHCO_3$). The vinegar is going to receive the baking soda and react. You don't need to understand the ion transfer of chemistry ($NaHCO_3 + CH_3COOH$ becomes $CH_3COONa + H_2O + CO_2(g)$, or sodium acetate, water, and carbon dioxide) to see and know there is a reaction. From a visual perspective, you will see foaming in the jar. This isn't magic, it's simply the natural laws of chemistry. The vinegar didn't make a choice about foaming. The baking soda didn't decide to foam. It happens because of chemistry. Period.

One can take that illustration and make it exponentially more complicated by making the chemical soup the human brain. One can then bring other items to interact with the brain. The items might be chemicals like what one eats or breathes, that find their way into the bloodstream and then into the brain to interact with the chemicals already there. The items might be visual stimuli that enter the brain after being seen by the eyes and then transmitted into electrical properties that impress the stimuli onto the chemicals in the brain. There might be sound waves that enter the brain after being sensed by our eardrums. Skinner would say that these encounters simply react by the laws of nature with our sacks of chemicals to alter our chemical makeup. But according to Skinner, all of it is determined solely by laws of nature. There is no real choice for you or me.

For Skinner, *choice* is a nice-sounding word with no real meaning. Choice is an illusion. It is what people think they are exercising, but in reality, people are chemicals reacting to stimuli, no more, no less.

Skinner's position is a logical one for the worldview of "There is no God." After all, if humans are only sacks of chemicals, it takes some mental gymnastics to deduce that people somehow have become so developed that people are sacks of chemicals that "make choices." That is not to say that there aren't philosophers and scientists that haven't suggested ways that people can make choices without there being a God, but those arguments are constantly evolving because no argument is sustainable through science. The studies trying to show that people truly exercise choices are not consistent in their findings and do not produce any clarity on this issue.

Skinner was selected as the most eminent psychologist of the twentieth century (beating out Sigmund Freud, who placed third). But he ran into a buzz saw over his plainly written book. The problem was that Skinner's position is consistent with his worldview that there is no God, but Skinner's position was not borne out of science or reality. There simply is no science to substantiate his views, and there is a lot of personal experience that weighs against it. From an early time, the problems with Skinner's view were pointed out by MIT's Noam Chomsky. Chomsky decried the speculative nature of Skinner's argument pointing out its lack of a scientific base.

> Since his William James lectures of 1947, Skinner has been sparring with these and related problems. The results are nil. . . . No scientific hypotheses with supporting evidence have been produced to substantiate the extravagant claims to which he is addicted. . . . Now we have virtually no scientific evidence and not even the germs of an interesting hypothesis about how human behavior is determined.[1]

Skinner was not deterred by his lack of science. Skinner believed that science just needed to catch up to his conclusions.

So, for Skinner, and others of his perspective, there is no dignity in any human person or action. Those like Skinner might go see *Man of La Mancha* and be moved as Don Quixote sings "The Impossible Dream." Or maybe they would be inspired to exercise watching Sylvester Stallone in the Rocky movies (at least the first two!). But in the end, inspired reactions are chemicals in the laws of nature cloaked as a value. The soldier who gives up her or his life for cause or country isn't doing anything worthy of praise or honor. That soldier is a sack of chemicals reacting by laws of nature. The soldier didn't really have a "choice." There is nothing that is noble. Sacrifice isn't noble, it is what a chemical grouping does when the chemicals and stimuli are just right.

Humans have come up with words and ideas like *responsibility*, *credit*, *respect*, *honor*, and *dishonor*, but to Skinner, those are labels without real meaning. No one is more worthy of respect than anyone else. Just because nature made one jar of vinegar larger than another, such that it reacts more prolifically to the baking soda doesn't give the jar a right to boast.

If Skinner's presuppositions are correct, if Skinner rightly interprets reality, that there is no God and humanity is a bag of chemicals, then his conclusions are consistent. Everything and everyone is just stardust residue put into self-contained chemical bags that react by the laws of nature, just as vinegar with soda.

Juxtaposed to Skinner's idea is the existence of a real God. The Judeo-Christian view of God that I set out in chapter two paints a much different view. The Judeo-Christian God created a world of cause and effect. The world of nature has cause and effect. If you drop a plate, gravity dictates it will fall. If it is sufficiently fragile, and a great enough force is exerted, it will break. This is cause and effect. This allows one to see elements of truth in the cause-and-effect ideas of Skinner. Because everyone lives in such a world, some people will have DNA that sets out their brain's chemical composition to be much different from that of others. This will cause different effects in how they act. But it is not the *only* source of their actions.

In addition to DNA and laws of nature, the Judeo-Christian view of reality sets out the ability of people to make choices that are truly choices. This is no illusion. Life is not predetermined. There is an ability to choose to eat the tuna sandwich or the pastrami on rye. One can decide what to watch on television or decide instead to read a book. The soldier has a choice about whether to fall on a grenade and save others. God has given humanity the ability to make these choices.

One sees this concept of cause and effect in the earliest pages of Hebrew Christian Scriptures. In the story of the Garden of Eden, God tells Adam and Eve not to eat the fruit from one certain tree, the tree of knowledge of good and evil. They are told that if they choose to eat of that tree, then they will die. Plainly, Adam and Eve have a choice. They can choose whether to eat from that tree. Yet also shown in that story is that if they eat, there will be consequences over which they have no choice. There is cause and effect from their actions, even though their actions are self-generated and not simply cause and effect from chemistry.

This view sets people apart from the rest of nature. People are not simply predetermined chemical robots. People aren't programmed by cause and effect. People can *cause effects* by real choices and actions. This is another aspect of the Judeo-Christian teaching that people are made in God's image. God is the ultimate "cause," ascribed as the one who set the laws of nature into motion. God is the one who caused all things to exist. One can trace all of nature's cause and effects back to God as the "first cause." Humanity, while not going back to a status as first cause, are still made in God's image and hence able to set up or create new causes and effects. If I choose to drive while sleepy, and fatigue causes a lapse in judgment and a car crash that kills an innocent bystander, I can set off effects that reverberate throughout time.

This aspect of life infuses dignity into actions (as well as indignity). It gives meaning to noble deeds. It inspires pride and appreciation for jobs well done. It finds values in altruistic behavior. It explains why dignity and honor are not hollow illusions but real values. It means people carry responsibility for their deeds. It makes sense of me, the people around me, and the world. It tells me that we are not living deluded in Illusionville but are truly experiencing real life. It is a further piece of evidence for me that weighs in on the side of scales that there is a God.

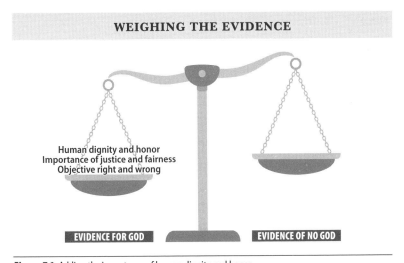

Figure 7.1. Adding the importance of human dignity and honor

WHY DO PEOPLE UNIQUELY VALUE HUMANITY?

I don't know any cannibals. Some think of cannibals as those among certain small tribes in the Amazon or some other unexposed pocket of the globe. Others may think of Hannibal Lecter in *The Silence of the Lambs*. Or Jeffrey Dahmer, the mass murderer. All of those, however, are considered the outskirts of society or the deranged among society. No one expects to find cannibals sitting in the PTA meeting or at the block party.

Yet there are many at PTA meetings and block parties who do not believe in the existence of God. Upon close examination, I find this doesn't make sense. The worldview that says there is no God should not have issues with consuming human chemicals for nourishment. It is a logical thing to do. To a thoughtful person who considers the implications of worldviews, those who believe there is no God should align closely with those advocating the consumption of human flesh.

I was once debating an atheist on British radio, both on and off the air. The atheist had a high view of human value, which I alleged was not based on his belief system but based on mine. I explained that his atheistic belief system gave no special value to humanity beyond being a sophisticated bag of chemicals, something he was hard-pressed to deny as an intellectual proposition. I then pressed, telling him that his high view of human value was a vestige from his days as a believer in God. He didn't like that. He pointed out to me that there are those who have a high view of human value that never believed in God, something I was wanting to hear from him.

At this point it allowed me to take the discussion down a specific road. I told him that under the view of reality given by the Judeo-Christian Scriptures, humanity *does have value*. Whether one recognizes it or not, people are made in God's image and are stamped with great intrinsic worth and value. It sets humanity apart from the rest of the animal kingdom. It makes people different. If the Judeo-Christian view is right, then most everyone, even those who don't believe in God, are going to be stamped with the awareness of the unique value of humanity.

As he challenged my conclusion, I asked him whether he or any of his atheist friends and colleagues were cannibals. He was taken back a bit as he answered, "Of course not!" I asked, "Why not?" He said he wasn't going to kill another person and eat them. When I added that I wasn't suggesting he kill anyone, but that people die for all kinds of reasons, and my question was whether he would eat humans. I then asked if he was a vegetarian, sparing all life from death or whether this was just something he didn't do for people. He said that he didn't eat those who had "higher consciousness."

Rather than debate the merits of what is high consciousness versus low consciousness, I pushed him on a glaring weakness in his argument. I said, "What about your grandmother. If she was lying in a hospital, and she was brain-dead. The doctors told you she had no consciousness and would never recover any. You are being told to pull the plug. Then would you do something with all the protein and vitamins in your grandmother's body, or would you let it go to waste? With all the people starving, would you donate her body as a food source?"

At this point, he made some comment about health issues associated with people eating people. I sidestepped that medical debate and instead pointed out he could feed his grandmother's corpse to a pig, and then the pig could be food for people. He would have nothing to do with it, but as much as I pressed him, he could never give me a logical reason why not. He couldn't tell me why; he just knew it wasn't right!

People place a unique value on humans. It doesn't make any sense to me under a worldview where there is no God. Yes, one can say that people with a higher consciousness might be worthy of some greater deference, but that doesn't explain why one values those of a lesser state. Yet, value them we do. If I go back to the creatures closely associated with humans, for example, the Neanderthals, there is good evidence that cannibalism was common. Of course, in the animal world, cannibalism is common. In the wild, monkeys account for 80 percent of a chimpanzee's kills for food.[2] Pigs will eat pigs. Lots of animals will eat their young. But modern humans see and understand a value in other modern humans that precludes such behavior.

Why? From a biblical perspective I see that somewhere amid all animals, a special human man and woman were endowed with the unique imprint of God's image. It was unique, such that the man (Adam) was unable to find a mate among all the other animals (including Neanderthals, if they were around!). Adam needed someone like him, someone in the image of God, able to relate, carrying God's moral thumbprint, able to create, and more. So, Adam is provided Eve, and modern humanity is birthed.

This is a compelling way that I see most everyone's life as consistent with the Judeo-Christian view of humanity, rather than that of humanity being only a patchwork of chemicals from cosmic stardust.

This has important implications for where one finds that value in people. There have been civilizations that are not based on Judeo-Christian principles that do think it appropriate to extinguish the life of those who are not as fit, not as smart, not similar in appearance, and so on. Yet the Judeo-Christian faith asserts that this is a distortion of humanity's true value and worth. Even though the exceptions exist beyond the Judeo-Christian sphere of influence, those civilizations and cultures still acknowledge the inherent unique value of humanity, but they just classify some as "subhuman." This, again, is evidence to me for the existence of God, as understood in Judeo-Christian Scripture.

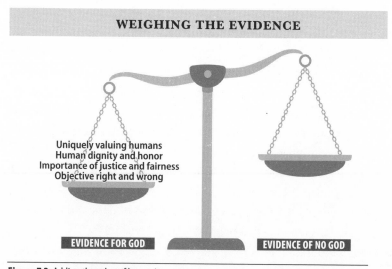

WEIGHING THE EVIDENCE

Uniquely valuing humans
Human dignity and honor
Importance of justice and fairness
Objective right and wrong

EVIDENCE FOR GOD   EVIDENCE OF NO GOD

Figure 7.2. Adding the value of humanity

WHY DO PEOPLE SEEK MEANING AND SIGNIFICANCE IN LIFE?

Something fundamental drives human thought and life. People are seekers by nature. People seek to know things. People seek to figure things out. People seek to love and to be loved. People seek companionship. People seek meaning and purpose.

As I ask why, I am confronted again by the two worldviews represented on the two sides of the scales. Is this drive to uncover meaning and significance in life one I would expect to find in a world where there is no God, or in one where there is a God?

To me, the answer lies in large part in whether the questions are real or fake. Of course, if there is no God, the cosmic significance of understanding life is zero. That the chemicals in my brain understand that the hydrogen molecules collected into a mass a few million miles away from the hydrogen atoms in my body are experiencing molecular fusion is really of no note. Those molecules will fuse whether I am aware of it. In other words, the sun doesn't quit shining just because I can't figure out what it is.

Yet when I talk to most anyone of intellectual accomplishment, I find them getting some measure of satisfaction in what they have learned or figured out. One can't read the writings of even the atheists like Dawkins without seeing their innate pleasure and satisfaction over figuring things out and being "in the know."

Philosopher and atheist Thomas Nagel has a chapter in his book *The View from Nowhere* titled "Birth, Death, and the Meaning of Life." This chapter touches me as Nagel struggles to understand meaning in life while stuck in a worldview where there is no God—just cosmic stardust.

Nagel begins the chapter with a compassionate story of a spider who died after Nagel "rescued" it from the urinal where the spider had lived for months. In the spider's death, Nagel saw a parable. It illustrates the hazards of combining perspectives that are radically different.[3]

Nagel is facing a dilemma. He wants an objective value and ethic as well as meaning in life. But starting with his own views, he knows the effort of seeking an objective value might lead to nihilism and meaninglessness. If there is a God, life can be meaningful, having a purpose and value. Without God, however, one can readily lapse into the absurdity expounded by Albert Camus (1913–1960). Journalist, playwright, novelist, activist, and philosopher all rolled into one, Camus's works embodied the paradox of people seeking meaning in a meaningless world.

In Camus's seminal work *The Myth of Sisyphus*,[4] Camus admits the essential meaninglessness of life, even while humanity constantly tries to find meaning. Camus wrote of the Greek myth of Sisyphus, who the gods had condemned to an eternity of rolling a massive stone uphill, only to have the boulder repeatedly roll back down as he approached the top. For Camus, this was the human paradox. People seek meaning, only to find there is none. People then seek it again anyway, as Sisyphus again struggled to get the boulder uphill.

History has been interesting to Camus. Camus's "meaning," if such could be labeled, was taking joy in accepting that one will search of meaning in a meaningless world. Yet in the decades since, even as philosophers pointed out that meaning in meaninglessness is an absurdity, many have continued the mission to find meaning in life, while still embracing an atheist worldview. Yet each attempt seems equally as hollow to me on examination.

Return to Nagel as an example. Nagel sees the problems from two perspectives. One he calls the "outer perspective." If one steps out of themselves to get a detached view of life and meaning, birth becomes "accidental," life is "pointless," and death is "insignificant." Nagel doesn't use my terms of "sacks of chemicals" and "cosmic stardust." Instead, he calls objective reality, existence, an "organic bubble" in a "universal soup."[5] Yet inside, Nagel knows this can't be it. His "inner perspective" shouts "my never having been born seems nearly unimaginable, my life monstrously important, and my death catastrophic."[6]

Nagel puts his finger on a problem—a problem for which he has no solution. The shoe doesn't fit. Let me describe it as I would at trial:

Nagel's objective truth as an atheist: There is no God. People are exceedingly temporary organic bubbles in a universal soup. There is no real meaning or value in anyone's existence.

Nagel's subjective reality as a human: Life must have meaning. People know it intrinsically. People are important and life has purpose.

Nagel's conclusion: These objective and subjective views are in conflict, and there is no credible way to eliminate the conflict. However, people should try to reduce the conflict by acknowledging it and living with subjective meaning.[7]

Nagel's problem and solution boil down to living the subjective lie, despite the objective truth. Perhaps this is in hope that one day someone figures out how his objective and subjective views can harmonize. But they can't. Two plus two can't equal fifteen. I think this is compelling evidence that reality is different than Nagel's worldview. While this drive for meaning and significance will never be understood by the cosmic-space-dust/sack-of-chemicals view of life, it makes total sense considering the Judeo-Christian God.

If I try to isolate the quest for meaning to the cosmic-dust view of humanity, then I am left with trying to figure out how the illusion of significance and purpose came to be, by all accounts, uniquely in humans. The device of natural selection might seem sensible here. It makes some sense that creatures who believe, even mistakenly, in purpose and who strive for significance will be most fit for the environment and most likely to propagate and live. Yet before I even get to natural selection, I am forced to confront the idea that somewhere DNA started registering the conscious thought of significance and purpose.

How and when DNA did this, science can't say. Maybe one day, it will unfold a "significance gene," but that gene has not yet been found. Of course, science can determine what regions of the brain are involved in the drive for significance and meaning, but that is not the same thing. I must also note, that should science find a "significance gene," such would not force a view of "no God." Certainly, the Judeo-Christian God works through DNA, and there are unanswered questions of where and how God instills purpose and meaning in people. He might well do it through DNA.

But regardless of how science finds the genesis of significance and meaning, the question that I think can be answered today is this: Does one believe that there really is significance and meaning? In other words, is it a semantic trick the mind is playing? Are people thinking about things that are illusory? If so, why doesn't the realization of it solve the puzzle? Why do people still have the drive after realizing the drive is fake? Why do people still search for meaning if they know it is meaningless? This doesn't make sense to me. I'm not saying it's not possible to be so deluded, but it defies common sense.

The Judeo-Christian alternative, however, fits experience like a solution to a puzzle. The Judeo-Christian view teaches that people were made to be in a relationship with God. In the earliest Scriptures, in the story of the Garden of Eden God walked with Adam and Eve, speaking with them in a real relationship. This was made possible in unique ways because God made people in his image, able to relate. The Christian addition to the Hebrew Scriptures adds the concept that God himself is capable of relationship within God. This is the Christian idea of God being three, even as he is one (the Trinity).

So from a Judeo-Christian perspective, people were made in the image of God to be in relationship with God. They had purpose; they had meaning; they had significance. Yet the story in the Garden says that Adam and Eve violated the relationship with God in a way that marred the relationship. Sin came into the picture. People chose to do things that were inconsistent with God's morality. In common parlance one might say, "They went somewhere God wouldn't go!" That resulted in the biblical metaphor of humanity "falling" from God.

In the Judeo-Christian teaching, that leaves people searching for something they don't have. People were made to be in a relationship that was lost. People were made for a significance they don't enjoy. It drives people to find it. It is the explanation for the deep-seated realization of people that, "There's got to be more to life than this."

The Christian thinker Augustine (354-430) wrote, "You have made us for yourself, and our heart is restless until it finds rest in you."[8] And the Christian rabbi Paul told the people of Athens midway through the first century that

> the God who made the world and everything in it, being Lord of heaven and earth, does not live in temples made by man, nor is he served by human hands, as though he needed anything, since he himself gives to all mankind life and breath and everything. And he made from one man every nation of mankind to live on all the face of the earth, having determined allotted periods and the boundaries of their dwelling place, that they should seek God, and perhaps feel their way toward him and find him. Yet he is actually not far from each one of us. (Acts 17:24-27)

The French polymath Blaise Pascal (1623–1662) was a mathematician, physicist, inventor, writer, and philosopher. In writing his thoughts on the Christian faith, he probed ideas on why people strive so hard to find happiness. He explained,

> What is it then that this desire and this inability proclaim to us, but that there was once in man a true happiness of which there now remain to him only the mark and empty trace, which he in vain tries to fill from all his surroundings, seeking from things absent the help he does not obtain in things present? But these are all inadequate, because the infinite abyss can only be filled by an infinite and immutable object, that is to say, only by God Himself.
>
> He only is our true good, and since we have forsaken Him, it is a strange thing that there is nothing in nature which has not been serviceable in taking His place; the stars, the heavens, earth, the elements, plants, cabbages, leeks, animals, insects, calves,

serpents, fever, pestilence, war, famine, vices, adultery, incest. And since man has lost the true good, everything can appear equally good to him, even his own destruction, though so opposed to God, to reason, and to the whole course of nature.

Some seek good in authority, others in scientific research, others in pleasure.[9]

I see here a ready explanation for the drive to meaning, but I must ask, What if this is an illusion? What if this is simply the drive discussed in the stardust model as natural selection happening upon it accidentally, and seizing it as a trait worth propagating?

My response is somewhat personal, but no less real. My response is that I, and many like me, who have found in their faith a restoration of the relationship with "God," have found the peace of satisfaction in significance and meaning. It is as if the hunger that drove me to find "something that is missing" has been satisfied. I know meaning. I know significance. I know purpose.

I work to learn and to love, not because I am driven blindly, but because I know what role it takes and where it fits. I learn because God has a world that is at my disposal, and I am told to try to use that world's laws to make it a better place. I am told to fight disease, misfortune, pain, and more by creatively using the resources of nature. If I can find a cure for cancer, I am doing a good thing. If I can mend a broken heart, I am doing a good thing. These are jobs of meaning and significance because they are part of my relationship with God, whose will and kingdom I desire.

It is a framework that explains my own significance and the drive for significance and purpose of others. It makes more sense to me than being cosmic space dust in a form left with chemical imprints of significance from other space dust.

In conclusion, because only the Judeo-Christian worldview makes sense to me on this issue, I place it in the scales on the side of "God."

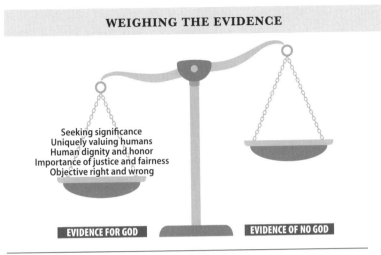

Figure 7.3. Adding the drive for significance

WHY DO MY ACTIONS FAIL TO MEET MY STANDARDS?

The Smithsonian National Museum of Natural History teaches that "early humans first migrated out of Africa into Asia probably between 2 million and 1.8 million years ago. They entered Europe somewhat later, between 1.5 million and 1 million years."[10]

If this is so, then I have a major beef with my historical relatives. They have had 2 million years, or if the average adult has children at age twenty-five, well over seventy-five thousand generations to naturally select people who do not overeat! I know, there is likely an argument that high-caloric food was not so readily available that all generations had an obesity issue, but I know it's been a problem for recorded history!

There are those who can eat anything they want, and they stay fit as a fiddle. I know. I have seen them. Then there are those who can smell the brownies in the oven and add five pounds before they come out. Now some will say, and I can see the logic, that the ability to put on weight might have its advantages in history when people needed to fatten during years of plenty to be able to sustain the years of famine. But it isn't only the body's reaction to food that concerns me. The real concern is something a bit deeper. It is the body's enslavement to, in some cases, overeating. It is the failure to develop the self-discipline so that one can readily choose whether it is a season to add pounds.

This is not simply a "digestion of the food" issue. Why haven't people developed the self-control that would allow everyone to make conscious decisions about what is best and then follow them? That is the real beef (pun intended) of my complaint.

With seventy-five thousand generations, it seems that humanity would have naturally selected those individuals who have the best self-control. Those are the ones who will live more successfully, who will be able to follow through on their decisions, who will be able to modify their behavior to meet the circumstances in a well-thought-out manner. Self-control and discipline seem to be traits that would surface fast through natural selection. It means people would be creatures who make decisions and find themselves able to follow through.

Now some have more self-control than others; that is without a doubt. Most everyone sees self-control as a virtue, an admirable trait that helps in life. Yet even those few with great self-control are not successful at doing all they want, at refraining from things they don't want, at controlling the urges of a baser nature. Why is that?

I weigh this issue in the scales I am using and consider the explanations for this reality considering there being no God versus the ideas of the Judeo-Christian God. My considerations here tilt the scales with the Judeo-Christian God being the better explanation, but only for some of the ideas. Let me explain.

On the issue of eating, I can see the historical advantages in different cultures and ages to having bodies that put on weight more readily than others. Having that trait, and the inability to control eating, could easily be a vestige of natural selection in that regard.[11] Those who were able to put on weight, intentionally or not, made it through times of famine and inadequate food sources to continue breeding and continue life.

Similarly, consider those who are unable to control their hormones shouting "Reproduce!" even though their minds are saying, "Not supposed to happen right now!" That lack of self-control might be the solution in a godless nature that has seen human beings continue to propagate.

But there are other issues of self-control that don't so readily meet the mold. There are times where I don't measure up to being the kind of worker I want or need to be. There are times where my parenting is less than it should be. There are times where I am not the kind of husband I would like to be. There are times where I would like to be a better friend. Sometimes I say things I don't want to say. Sometimes I fail to say or do things that I should say or do. Sometimes I lose my cool.

Can I imagine ways that these traits *might* have a better result than the trait of self-control? Of course! But those are the exceptions. In the main, these are traits that should have been weeded out thousands of generations ago! It doesn't make sense to me in weighing the scales that poor self-control would be explained by the absence of God.

What is the Judeo-Christian explanation for this reality of life? Does the Judeo-Christian explanation make sense of humanity's experience in the arena of poor self-control?

The biblical account that explains the condition of humanity is first told in the story of the Garden of Eden. God had two perfectly formed humans in the Garden, able to make real choices (what to eat and whom to obey), create from their imaginations (naming animals), work toward goals (tend the garden), and relate harmoniously in personal and real terms (to God and with each other).

God instructed and warned both that if they made a certain choice to disobey God, and to eat of a certain forbidden tree, the consequences would be devastating. Ultimately the result would be the death penalty. The two people, Adam and Eve, lived for some unknown period in the harmony and opportunity afforded by God's bountiful paradise. Then something changed.

An enemy of God and of people slithered into Eve's presence and got her to question God's instructions. The enemy was able to persuade her to defy God, and she chose to make her own rules. She made the deliberate choice to eat the forbidden fruit and then got her husband to do the same.

The consequences were, literally and figuratively, of biblical proportions. There was an immediate displacement in the relationship between Adam, Eve, and God. The harmony was gone. Adam and Eve hid from God. When confronted, Adam blamed Eve, then blamed God (for providing Eve). There was shame and awareness of violating God's instructions (a.k.a. sin). Death set in. In part this was a physical degradation process that would pass on to all generations proceeding from Adam and Eve, but it was also a death "inside." It meant that Adam and Eve were darkened in their ability to discern right and wrong, to do right and wrong, to be who they were made to be, doing what they were made to do. It put enmity between them and each other, them and God, and them and the earth. They were no longer in a paradise but would have to find a way to live among thorns and thistles.

God explained this condition of death as they were expelled from his presence in the garden of perfection, "Cursed is the ground because of you; in pain you shall eat of it all the days of your life; thorns and thistles it shall bring forth for you; and you shall eat the plants of the field. By the sweat of your face you shall eat bread, till you return to the ground, for out of it you were taken; for you are dust, and to dust you shall return" (Gen 3:17-19).

Adam and Eve's actions brought this about. It left them less than they were made to be. They longed for relationships that were not marred or destroyed. They had to sweat to make things work when those things had previously come as gifts. It took the pleasures of work and turned them into sweat and toil.

There are many other places where the Bible expands on this teaching, with the Christian/Jewish lawyer Paul writing, "Sin came into the world through one man, and death through sin, and so death spread to all men because all sinned. . . . Because of one man's trespass, death reigned through that one man" (Rom 5:12, 17).

According to the biblical account, people are made for something greater. People are made to be in a moral relationship with a moral God. Yet no one can do so. Everyone was born into the condition of sin, which mars the ability to live perfectly. Try as one might, no one has the mind for it, the self-control for it, or the emotional drive for it. Everyone falls short of what one wants. People are sinners, living out the death sentence promised beforehand to the progenitors.

So people may want to do right, but with every generation, people will not find any who can live as they want. I have yet to see a child who needs lessons in how to disobey. All children come by that naturally. Parents must teach them obedience. Parents must teach them to do right.

Admittedly this is a personal issue with people, but as I experience this reality, the biblical account gives a very reasonable explanation to me for how I am, and how you are.

Before I proceed to the next group of evidence, I need to account for another aspect of people not measuring up to the standards one expects or desires. To this point, I have considered most people who are "inadequate" and lacking in self-control. But there is a whole other set of people whose actions do not measure up to standards. These are the evil people who haunt our world. They are the kidnappers, rapists, murderers. The generals who lead armies to destroy people groups. The Maos, Hitlers, and Stalins in our world who oversee the deaths of tens of millions of people.

Why do these people still find power and support in this world? Why are they able to live and perpetrate their evil? The examination given above actually applies to these people as well. I suspect most have either lost self-control (rapists, for example), or they have become so deluded that they have justified their atrocities somehow in their minds. Of course, the Christian explanation makes great sense, both for the lack of self-control and for the delusion of zealotry that accompanies warped standards of behavior. But beyond that, about those who are evil, one must ask the hard question, Why does God, if he exists and if he is a good God, allow such evil to exist?

I consider this in the next group of evidence, but first, I add to my scales the evidence of failing to meet my standards.

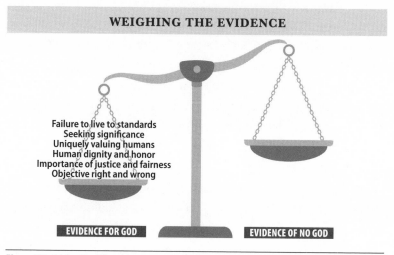

Figure 7.4. Adding the failure to meet my standards

8

THE PROBLEM OF SUFFERING

TRIAL WORK TAKES A GREAT DEAL of time and effort. Good trial lawyers always assess evidence that belies their position as well as supportive evidence. That's because truth doesn't pick and choose facts. All facts fit into the true story. The accurate picture can't be found without integrating all relevant evidence. Considering the evidence about God's existence should be no different.

At this point, I am shifting to those pieces of evidence I have grouped under "negative perceptions and questions." These are areas and arguments set out by many agnostics and atheists who have abdicated any faith in God (or gods).

WHY IS THERE SUFFERING?

One of Christianity's bestselling critics is Bart Ehrman. In a popular bestseller challenging the authenticity of the Christian faith and the validity of the Bible as an authoritative text, Ehrman wrote, "If there is an all-powerful and loving God in this world, why is there so much excruciating pain and unspeakable suffering? The problem of suffering has haunted me for a very long time. . . . Ultimately, it was the reason I lost my faith."[1]

Ehrman wrote of a Christmas Eve service he attended where this issue of suffering moved him away from faith. The service's prayer was for God, who came into the darkness of the world bringing light through the life of the divine Christ child, to come into the world of darkness again today.

Ehrman explained,

> Where is this God now? If he came into the darkness and made a difference, why is there still no difference? Why are the sick still wracked with unspeakable pain? Why are babies still born with birth defects? Why are young children kidnapped, raped, and murdered? Why are there droughts that leave millions starving, suffering horrible and excruciating lives that lead to horrible and excruciating deaths? If God intervened to deliver the armies of Israel from its enemies, why doesn't he intervene now when the armies of sadistic tyrants savagely attack and destroy entire villages, towns, and even countries? If God is at work in the darkness, feeding the hungry with the miraculous multiplication of loaves, why is it that one child—a mere child!—dies every five seconds of hunger? Every five seconds.[2]

This is a common view, and a piece of evidence I take very seriously. I have considered it for forty years, and as I turn over the evidence and consider the implications, I keep returning to the same conclusion. This is actually evidence that supports the Judeo-Christian view of God, not evidence against it. Here is my reasoning.

Suffering is real. Suffering is horrible. Suffering is brutal and makes me angry and frustrated. It can bring tears to my eyes. I have seen sweet and innocent young people die. Does this mean there is no God? Of course not! Consider the options: Maybe there is no God (Ehrman's conclusion). Maybe there is a God, but he is evil and malevolent (actually the view of some I've met). There might be a callous God. There might be a God who ignores earth (the Deist's view). There might be a God who is not all-powerful. With due respect to Ehrman, the presence of suffering doesn't indicate there is no God, but it *might* indicate that the loving and all-powerful Judeo-Christian God is not real. That is where my examination turns.

To properly examine this issue, one should consider what *kind* of God would exist to explain suffering, what *kind* of world would explain suffering, and what *kind* of humanity would explain suffering.

Before examining the questions above, I think one thing should be underscored. Suffering bothers people, especially when it is deemed "unfair." One might be okay with soldiers being killed in a just war, but the collateral damage of a schoolhouse full of children being killed causes great consternation.

That the suffering of others bothers people so much must be considered as possible evidence for God's existence. This also calls into play the consideration of why there is a basis for dignity and honor as well as why people value humanity and find meaning and significance in life. At the end of the day, the mere fact that suffering is so bothersome is a strong indication that people are something more than human chemical sacks. If people weren't wired somehow to understand and appreciate justice, no one would be so concerned over the suffering of innocents.

WHAT KIND OF GOD COULD EXPLAIN THE SUFFERING?

For some reason I can't understand, some people believe that whatever is their concept of God, that must be what or who God really is. I often hear of people saying God is "omnipotent," meaning "all-powerful." Whether or not that is a biblical truth, however, depends upon what someone means by "all-powerful." What the theologian means by God being omnipotent isn't what a lot of others mean when they speak of omnipotence.

Let me give an example. When I was in about fourth grade, I asked my mother if I could make the brownies from the mix I found in the kitchen. Mom told me, "Yes, just follow the instructions." I did. Mom walked in on me at the point where I had my hands in the mixing bowl, squeezing the batter through my fingers. Mom laughingly asked me what on earth I was doing. I replied, "Following the recipe! It said to 'Mix by hand.'" In my mind, I thought that was what Mom did with meatloaf, and so I was doing the same.

Like the brownie instructions to mix by hand, *omnipotent* might mean one thing to one while another thing to another. The Bible refers to God as "all-powerful" or "almighty" in both the Hebrew Scriptures ("Old Testament") and the New Testament Scriptures of the Christian faith. The Hebrew used a word *shaddai*, which was considered a name of God, related to the ancient Arabic root that speaks of "strength." Indeed, God is "strong." In the New Testament, the word used is *pantokrator*, which conveys the idea of "all-powerful," but that's not the whole story. Here is where one can make some mistakes in understanding.

The early Jewish Christians that were writing the New Testament often used a Greek translation of the Hebrew Bible. Jewish scholars made this Greek translation (called the Septuagint) before the birth of Jesus. The Greek version of the Hebrew Scriptures did *not* use the word *pantokrator* or "all-powerful" to translate the Hebrew for *shaddai*, or "strong." The Greek "all-powerful" translated the Hebrew *tseva'ot*, referring to "hosts" or "armies." God is "all-powerful" in the biblical sense that he has dominion over all the hosts. The Latin church took this Greek idea and turned it into the Latin word *omnipotens*, from which is derived *omnipotent*.

What is the point of this language discussion? The meaning behind words is critical if one is to make brownies *or* to understand that there may be a difference between who people think God is and who God actually is. There might also be a difference between what people *want* God to be and what God is.

So on the issue of God being all-powerful, people do an injustice to the concept of the Judeo-Christian God if they think that means, for example, that God can make two plus two equal fifteen. That is not what *all-powerful* means. *All-powerful* places God above the hosts. It makes him the strong one who can do as he pleases. But it doesn't mean he can be something he's not. He can't make a rock he can't lift. This isn't because he isn't all powerful, but because the concept is an incoherent one.

In this sense, one might want God to be something God isn't. One might want God to be always making sure people are happy. One might want God to make people puppets and strip them of their free choice. (For example, some believe that God shouldn't allow people to get drunk and drive. They want a God who is the cosmic Breathalyzer or Intoxalock.) People might want God to make the world Harry Potter–esque, stopping the laws of nature when there might otherwise be a hurricane or flood. In that regard, people might also want God to stop any human influence on global warming, which itself, according to most models of science, leads to extremes of weather occurrences. Maybe someone wants God to be a cosmic vaccine to stop the spread of disease. Or perhaps people expect God to be cosmic birth control, stopping all sperm from people who will be bad dads from entering the ova of people who will be bad mothers. Or should God be the cosmic bullet-proof vest, to stop the laws of nature that allow gunshot wounds?

Taken to an extreme, maybe some want God to stop anyone from dying, so everyone can live forever on this earth, restoring Eden. In the end, maybe some might want a God who wouldn't make people at all, if it meant that some people would be bad and choose to work against God instead of for him.

Could God do these things? Technically, I guess he could, but not in this world he has made. That would not be a real world with real choices. It would be a puppet world where all choices are dictated by God, the cosmic equivalent of a computer game where God does all the programming, and humanity is simply a family living in a simulated universe. No one can exist in such a world if people have freedom to make choices. It is as illogical as two plus two equaling fifteen.

A God who stops everything negative is not a reasonable expectation. It certainly isn't the biblical God. I believe it is a naive view that is not fully thought through. Not wanting to offend anyone who speaks like this, I will explain why it seems to me that the reasoning used is typically quite superficial. The reasoning sounds like a high school debate class: "If God is God, then God can do anything. If God can do anything, then God can make a world where this doesn't happen." Or "If God can do anything, then God can intervene whenever anything bad is going to happen." That may sound logical, but it isn't. It makes no more sense than, "God can't exist, because if he did, then he could make a rock he couldn't lift. But then if he couldn't lift it, he wouldn't be all-powerful. So, there must not be a God."

No, God cannot make a rock he cannot lift. That simply isn't possible or logical. There are lots of things that are illogical and impossible for God. God's character is that of a consistent and unchanging God. He can't become inconsistent. He can't become sinful. He can't cease to exist. He can't get sick. He can't have accidents. There is a lot that is not in the realm of possible for God. That doesn't make him less God.

The biblical God exists as a specific being, united as one, though finding expression in what is often best understood as "three persons." This biblical God was able to make people with the ability to make their own moral choices. People can choose to treat others with kindness and charity; people can choose to treat others contemptuously or with cruelty. People can choose to help those who need help; people can choose to take advantage of others. People can choose to feed the hungry; people can choose to let them starve. People can choose to live destructively; people can choose to live constructively. People can choose to slaughter innocents; people can choose to protect others.

These are real choices. People have them. People can exercise them. People are responsible for them. God isn't. God should not be blamed for the poor or wicked choices of others. Do people want God to be the "don't let anything bad happen" police officer? Cruising around in a supernatural squad car patrolling for crimes about to be committed, and then bending the laws of nature to prevent them? That is not God, and that is not this world.

The biblical God is one who made the world, placed all sorts of living beings here (this is still not the time yet to discuss how he did so— evolution, intelligent design, or creation out of nothing), and among all the species, had one that was specially endowed to be in his image.

These primeval humans were given clear directions and told of consequences for bad choices. They made a choice and those consequences have happened. They are tragic. There is no disputing that.

The story after Adam and Eve were expelled from paradise illustrates this. Adam and Eve were injected into the world of thorns, thistles, pain, and other results from rebellion against God and his goodness. Into this world, they gave birth to two sons, Cain and Abel. As they got older, Cain and Abel were interfacing with God, and Cain's attitudes were wrong. God warned Cain that "sin [was] crouching" at his door. Cain was warned that he was close to doing some very wrong things that would have wrong consequences. After the experience of his parents, this should have put Cain on high alert. But no, it didn't. Instead, in a fit of envy and rage, Cain killed Abel, an innocent.

Did Abel deserve it? No. Did Abel commit the sin? No. This was Cain's sin, and both Cain and Abel suffered for it. Abel, one may assume in the biblical story suffered only momentarily. The Bible teaches that he was eternity bound and that death to one in God's care is a graduation, not an end. Cain's suffering was much longer than Abel's. It lasted Cain's whole life.

This story readily shows that God's charge to people to tend to the earth is a real charge (Gen 2:15). Humans have the ability to make choices that have real consequences. People can do good or do evil, and the choices have results. Giving this truly awesome responsibility to people does not mean God is evil. God is not the one doing the bad thing. God warns and teaches people what is right to do. Cain had no excuse. God warned him. Adam and Eve had no excuse. God warned them. But they had choices, and those choices had real consequences. Is God really to blame for making us such significant beings? As my friend Dr. Michael Lloyd wrote, "Personally, I find it helpful to think that our freedom to make choices that have huge consequences is what makes us significant beings. If nothing depended on the decisions we make, if our choices didn't really make any difference, how significant would we be?"[3]

There is a redemptive side of the story. Generally, one does not see God taking the wicked or evil person and slamming destruction upon them at the first moment they do an evil deed. The Christian understanding is that God is wanting even the evilest people to change their minds and their behaviors (the biblical word is *repent*) and put their lives to use in service to God (2 Pet 3:9). This is not some pie-in-the-sky idea. One need only look at John Newton, the famous slave trader who changed his direction in life, becoming a devout Christian and writing the world-renowned hymn "Amazing Grace."

Even with the wicked choices of people, choices that bring death, God has promised and planned a route of redemption for people. On this path, the just consequence of sin and disobedience is met, it is not whitewashed. God doesn't excuse evil *sua sponte* (i.e., by itself without regard to anything else), but in a way where people can come back into a restored relationship with God based on *justice* as well as mercy. God doesn't roll back the consequences of sin/evil, but he meets them head on in a personal manner, and he takes the effects of sin/evil to his own detriment through the death of Jesus, so that others will not have to bear them.

Despite the suffering caused by sin/evil, the ultimate consequence (the death sentence) is removed, as that debt is paid by God himself. Shall I shake my fist to the skies and say, "How dare you, God? How dare you let this or that bad thing happen?" Well, I can, but I must remember the Judeo-Christian teaching that God didn't make this world for suffering. He had a much grander purpose.

God is at work trying to alleviate suffering. He has taught any who would listen to him that one's Christian responsibility is to be his vessel for reaching the world in his love and compassion. God's followers are to feed the hungry, clothe the naked, tend to the sick, fellowship with the lonely, and more. See the sternness of this teaching from Jesus who said,

> Then the King will say to those on his right, "Come, you who are blessed by my Father, inherit the kingdom prepared for you from

the foundation of the world. For I was hungry and you gave me food, I was thirsty and you gave me drink, I was a stranger and you welcomed me, I was naked and you clothed me, I was sick and you visited me, I was in prison and you came to me." Then the righteous will answer him, saying, "Lord, when did we see you hungry and feed you, or thirsty and give you drink? And when did we see you a stranger and welcome you, or naked and clothe you? And when did we see you sick or in prison and visit you?" And the King will answer them, "Truly, I say to you, as you did it to one of the least of these my brothers, you did it to me."

Then he will say to those on his left, "Depart from me, you cursed, into the eternal fire prepared for the devil and his angels. For I was hungry and you gave me no food, I was thirsty and you gave me no drink, I was a stranger and you did not welcome me, naked and you did not clothe me, sick and in prison and you did not visit me." Then they also will answer, saying, "Lord, when did we see you hungry or thirsty or a stranger or naked or sick or in prison, and did not minister to you?" Then he will answer them, saying, "Truly, I say to you, as you did not do it to one of the least of these, you did not do it to me." (Mt 25:34-45)

Now should God choose another method to use other than people? Should he have made this earth his paint canvas, simply grabbing some food paint to add where there are hungry people? Should he retract his instructions to his people and instead insert: "Hey, I want you to help those suffering, but no big deal if you don't. I will do it all myself." Again, that is not God making a world of autonomy with laws of nature and rules of life.

Then what of the argument that Ehrman and others make about God at times intervening? The Bible does say that God (Jesus) used a few loaves and fishes to feed thousands. The Hebrew celebration of *Pesach* ("Passover") is based on the biblical story of God intervening in laws of nature to bring the Israelites out of Egypt, miraculously parting the Reed Sea in the process (Ex 14).[4] The resurrection of Jesus from the dead certainly appears to have violated more than a few laws of nature.

Certainly, God can and does alter nature at times to effectuate his will. The biblical teaching recognizes that such things occur, but they happen rarely. God does so to effectuate his ultimate will. God will intervene as necessary to bring this world to its conclusion as promised by God. But more often one sees God working his will more obviously through the laws of nature, through the choices and actions of people, not apart from them.

In the law there is a doctrine of "constitutional avoidance." This doctrine says that when courts are ruling on matters, they should refuse to rule on a constitutional issue if the issue can be resolved on a non-constitutional basis. Is this because courts don't have the ability or authority to rule on constitutional issues? Of course not. They absolutely have that ability and authority. They are the only branch of government that can.

This judicial minimalism is important. Judicial review of the constitution is a potent tool that addresses not only the matter at hand but also can affect any future matter that might come along on any related subject. Courts recognize that the fallout from their decisions on other matters increases significantly with the breadth of judicial interference. For example, if a court is faced with a singular issue about whether one who is developmentally disabled with an IQ below 70 can be given the death penalty and the court finds that the trial was not conducted fairly, the court will refrain from writing on the entire issue of whether the death penalty violates the constitutional rights of one with that mental deficit. To quote the current chief justice of the United States Supreme Court when explaining a limited ruling, "This is a sufficient ground for deciding this case, and the cardinal principle of judicial restraint—if it is not necessary to decide more, it is necessary not to decide more—counsels us to go no further."[5]

Here is a good sound reasoning behind God's restraint as well. If one thinks of this world like a sudoku puzzle, tampering with one number will affect all others. Could God rid the world of disease with a snap of his supernatural fingers? Of course. Yet the impact would be profound. It could result in populations with insufficient food, inadequate housing, fighting over property and possessions, and unemployment ramifications when jobs never come open.

If one hasn't spent much time studying the science of economics, this might seem trivial, if even notable at all. It isn't. Economist Edwin Dolan makes the point forcefully in his book *TANSTAAFL (There Ain't No Such Thing as a Free Lunch)*. Dolan points out that at the root of the relationships between living beings and the environment, the science of ecology is based on the broad premise that "everything depends on everything else." Dolan then explains in economic terms,

> The theory of general economic equilibrium teaches us that a change in the price or quantity produced of any good or service will affect the price and quantity produced of all other goods and services. A decline in the production of cattle will result in a decreased supply of leather. Up will go the price of leather, and hence of leather shoes. Consumers will buy fewer leather and more synthetic shoes. Workers will be laid off in the tanneries and taken on in plastics mills. Real estate values will fall in the neighborhood of the former and rise in the neighborhood of the latter. Eventually—according to economic science this is a literal certainty limited only by our ability to measure—the impact will be felt upon the price of eggs in China.[6]

God has made a world for humans to negotiate and work. Adam and Eve were instructed to tend to the garden, to name the animals, and so on. This is the way the world is set up, and God's supernatural interventions come, but they come rarely. God exercises judicial restraint. For God to do otherwise, would strip the truth of the human role in life. It would make this world a charade, not a real world.

Yes, God could have made a lightning bolt strike Hitler right before he was elected. But the ramifications of that no one knows. Instead,

God worked through the efforts of valiant men and women, many of whom gave up their lives, to strip the world of the Third Reich and its devastating evil deeds, bringing Hitler to naught, and keeping this world on the course to seal up destiny within God's will. Does that mean there is no God for no God would have done so? No. It means that the biblical God worked in the manner of the biblical God. Is that the way I would do it if I were God? I suggest no one can answer that question. No one can say what would have happened to the world in the event Hitler was hit by lightning. There were plenty of evil people making evil choices in the Third Reich and elsewhere. Replace Hitler with another *Führer*—Raeder, Goebbels, or Himmler—and Germany might have won the war!

Yes, Jesus fed thousands with a few loaves and fishes. Should Jesus have done so daily, no doubt he would have alleviated hunger. He would also have put all the fishermen and bakers out of jobs. Then there would have been inadequate money for them to buy clothes and shelter. So maybe Jesus then clothes everyone and does supernatural carpentry to work on their homes? That then puts out of work those in the clothing industry and home building/repair. Of course, without people in the clothing industry, the wool needed from sheep is no longer purchased, and those reliant upon shepherding face a bleak future.

Or maybe God snaps his divine fingers at 8:00 p.m. tonight and cures cancer worldwide. Then all the oncologists tomorrow can be looking for new jobs, and all those working as technicians and all the related pharmaceutical workers and other affiliated industries are shut down. Of course, heaven forbid that God cures just cancer. What of those dying from coronaviruses? God should cure them as well. And then a host of other diseases that are killing people. Shouldn't God cure them also? What about those not dying from disease, but just hurting badly, or perhaps incapacitated? God should certainly cure them. In fact, there really shouldn't be any disease.

With all this, the entire health care sector can shut down, hospitals can lie empty, and the construction trades cease also. After all, who needs builders when there is God—because isn't that God also going to provide housing for the destitute? These people then quit spending the money they are no longer earning, and the economy begins to drag. Home loans are defaulted, bank loans go unpaid, and spending declines. Affiliated stock prices become worthless, and on and on, all creating more suffering that God is supposed to then snap his fingers and fix disease and hurt.

Therefore, I call this viewpoint naive. It fails to think through real implications and is more of a high school debate proposition.

WHAT KIND OF WORLD WOULD EXPLAIN THE SUFFERING?

So what kind of God would explain the suffering? A God who created human beings not as robots but as significant beings, able to make real decisions that have real consequences. But if that is the understanding of God that helps explain why the world is the way it is, it remains to ask what understanding of the world helps one understand its suffering and pain.

If I change my focus from the kind of God that would explain suffering and narrow it to the world's suffering of famine, hurricanes, and the like, I still weigh two models, one of no God and one of the Judeo-Christian God. If there is no God, what explains the suffering of this world? Are we on a cosmic dirt clod that is subject to harsh, uncaring laws of nature? That would certainly be possible. That might make sense in and of itself. The area where it doesn't make sense is how people react to the suffering brought on by the inanimate world.

The way humanity reacts to the suffering and how significantly it weighs on people poses a predicament. I might understand my repulsion for my own suffering. That is a mechanism that natural selection would want to ensure I have a good and full life, but the tragic nature of others' suffering is altogether different.

What reason would I have for caring if famine caused other people that are continents away to hurt with hunger or be treated unfairly?

In fact, to the extent that some are shorted in this life, it might provide more for others. If food availability is a zero-sum game, then maybe having a smorgasbord available to me as a result of others going hungry might seem good. That part of people that declares, "No, this is not right. No one should suffer needlessly!" is something that makes the most sense to me under the Judeo-Christian understanding of God having made humanity to reflect his care, compassion, and sense of justice.

If I consider the Judeo-Christian concept of God, I have a ready understanding of the world-induced suffering as well as our reaction to it. There is a world with its order, and it is not part of God. It is an independent creation of God. Humanity began that world in a garden paradise prepared by God. Humans are fashioned and endowed with abilities to accomplish their God-given task, that is, to tend the garden. While Adam and Eve walked in fellowship with God, all was well. There was no suffering. The world did not operate in a way that hurt them in the utopia of Eden. Then a corner was turned.

The Jewish/Christian Scriptures teach that Adam and Eve were beings with choice. The first chapter of the Bible says that God gave the names to darkness and light. God called the expanse "heavens" and gave to the seas their name (Gen 1:5-10). Then God made people in his image, and God assigned to Adam the task of naming the animals (Gen 2:19). God exercised the choice in Genesis 1; God assigned the choice to humanity in chapter two. Humans had choices, and their choices were real. The results of those choices were significant.

Adam and Eve made the deliberate choice to be their own gods, setting up their own boundaries and defining their own right and wrong. The temptation set before them was to disobey God with the assurance that their "eyes will be opened," and they would be "like God" (Gen 3:5). Adam and Eve were not puppets. They were real people with real choices that would have real consequences. When Adam and Eve chose rebellion, they lost life in paradise. They were ejected from Eden and sent into a fallen world to live the lives they chose.

The changes are set out in Genesis 3:17-19: "Cursed is the ground because of you; in pain you shall eat of it all the days of your life; thorns and thistles it shall bring forth for you; and you shall eat the plants of the field. By the sweat of your face you shall eat bread, till you return to the ground, for out of it you were taken; for you are dust, and to dust you shall return."

Post-Eden, humanity finds itself in a war zone, not a utopia. This is not rooted in God's uncaring nature; it is the real result of sin. Notice the curse is given "because of you." It came from the sins of Adam and Eve, not from the hand of God.

Meanwhile, humanity still understands that suffering is not good. God never made the world so that it would abuse people. This makes sense to me, not only because of its explanation of the world but also for its explanation of why so many care so much. I do care that others suffer in another continent, even though I will never know them. Furthermore, as the charge was given by Jesus to help those in need, the Christian understanding is that there are tools in the world that are at people's disposal to try and alleviate some of the pain and suffering brought about by the world.

This is part of the Christian understanding of science and medicine. Science, medicine, and the laws of nature give people tools to combat the suffering brought about by sin and the world. Humanity can use weather forecasting to move people out of the way of incoming hurricanes. People can work with fertilizers to make more food available. Inventors can develop machinery that can plow a field most efficiently to produce crops. Of course, the obverse is equally true. Humanity can choose not to do so. People can choose instead to use the tools of this world for destructive ends. The instructions of Jesus make clear God's charge to help others in need. That is the work of God through his people in this fallen world.

What kind of a world would explain the suffering within it? A world that is other than God, with its own order and integrity—a world

which free and significant agents can affect, for good or ill. This leads
to the next question.

WHAT KIND OF HUMANITY WOULD EXPLAIN THE SUFFERING?

There are people who cause suffering. Some bring about suffering on
a minor scale, while others do so on a monstrous level. Earlier I quoted
Ehrman's concern about "the armies of sadistic tyrants [that] savagely
attack and destroy entire villages, towns, and even countries."

Where does this depth of depravity come from? How can humans
be so inhumane? As I consider the two sides of the scales, I first look
at the evidence that this results from godless natural selection. Here I
return to my considerations of B. F. Skinner's hypothesis that people
are only genetics and the internal chemistry of exposure to environ-
mental actions. This would mean that those who cause suffering have
a DNA makeup that, when exposed to the influences of their experiences in life, determined the resulting behavior. I then remove this
behavior from personal accountability; after all, no one chooses their
DNA, and even if they did, that choice would likewise be dictated by
the laws of physics and chemistry. This is a chain that would go back
to the Big Bang.

This answer is fraught with the same concerns and problems I
outlined concerning Skinner's determinism. Additionally, though, it
is also troubled by the ideas behind a view of natural selection that
makes no room for God. As a species, if people are to procreate, re-
inforce, and refine themselves based on the traits that make them
most fit for the environment in which they are found, it seems
against common sense that those who carry the sadistic and inhumane traits would still be around after a few million years of
breeding. Surely natural selection would have gotten rid of those
DNA traits by now.

It might make some sense that the DNA traits that enable people to
win wars and exercise dominion over others will continue to flourish

as part of natural selection. But there are people who are marvelous leaders, who command respect, and who are models of virtue. The traits that make someone effective in battle or politics does not require degenerative behavior and evil.

It seems to me most reasonable to expect that these traits would be decreasing, if not fully eliminated by now. Yet look at the tyrants and wicked people in recent history. Saddam Hussein, Muammar Gaddafi, Pol Pot, Kim Jong-il, the people behind the Kosovo and Bosnia ethnic cleansings, not to mention the child molesters, the Sandy Hook and Columbine tragedies, and more—humanity hasn't been able to naturally select its way out of this evil.

On the Judeo-Christian side of the scale, there is a much different calculus. The Judeo-Christian position is that there will always be evil. There are people who live in rebellion against God. People who aren't in fellowship with God, even though hardwired for morality, are able to delude themselves, rally others in support, and do unspeakable horrors. The Judeo-Christian teaching is that these people are encouraged, enabled, and prodded by a level of unseen evil that finds expression in Satan and his demonic hordes. These forces work in bringing about evil and will never be eliminated by natural selection.

The Judeo-Christian explanation gives a source for the evil (fallen people influenced by evil forces) but also gives an answer for the evil. God has charged his followers to combat the evil on this earth. God has also promised fully and finally to vanquish and eliminate evil. Evil will be destroyed as the current order of the world comes to an end.

In vivid imagery, the New Testament book of Revelation recounts a vision given to a man named John that includes scenes of the final triumph of God over evil. The demonic forces are conquered, and the evildoers are punished and destroyed.

> The devil who had deceived them was thrown into the lake of fire and sulfur where the beast and the false prophet were, and they will be tormented day and night forever and ever. . . . This is the

second death, the lake of fire. And if anyone's name was not found written in the book of life, he was thrown into the lake of fire. (Rev 20:10, 14-15)

Some ask, if there is a God, why does he allow evil? Who made evil or where did it come from? The Christian faith explains evil as *the absence of or the marring of good*. For example, sexuality expressed in a faithful marital relationship is a good thing. It is a gift from God. But that same sexuality forced on someone, or perpetrated on a child or animal, is wrong and evil. Evil will always exist when people who can make choices choose evil. Evil is not "made" in the normal sense of the word. Evil is what happens when good is gone or mutilated. It is like turning off the light. When one turns off the light, there is darkness. The darkness wasn't "made." It was simply what happens when you remove light. In the same way, if you remove good, you are left with evil.

Evil deeds have evil consequences, even on good people. This is what stumps so many when they consider how that can be with a loving God. The Christian response is an important insight into reality. Unlike the non-God response that struggles with the reality of evil after millions of years of natural selection, the Christian response recognizes this world as a war zone, not a utopia. God wins the war, but people still must fight the battles. God calls on his followers to hate evil (Rom 12:9); to feed the hungry, clothe the naked, and aid the sick and imprisoned (Mt 25:34-40). God wants his followers to invoke his power to defeat the forces of evil (Mt 6:9-10) and to pray for those who are evil (Mt 5:43-45).

The Judeo-Christian view of reality says that there is a God who finds evil appalling, who tells his followers to fight against it, and who promises to ultimately destroy it and its perpetrators. This explains to me why I abhor evil. This explains why so many in the world want to fight against it. I do not find the idea that there is a loving God to be invalid in light of a world filled with evil. I find that a loving God explains it. It explains why I know evil is wrong. It explains why evil hasn't been diluted from the gene pool; it explains why I want to try and stop evil. It explains reality. I don't consider the presence of suffering as proof there is no God. I think it indicates there is a God, and it inspires me to fight as he has instructed me!

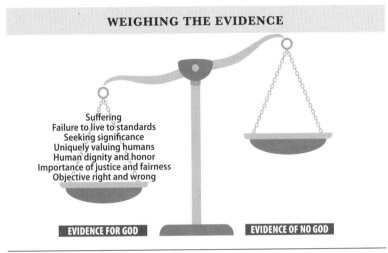

Figure 8.1. Adding the presence of suffering

9

THE INVISIBLE GOD

A SECOND ARGUMENT AGAINST GOD'S EXISTENCE is a deviation of an argument that I considered in chapter three.

WHY CAN'T I SEE GOD?

Many people ask this, even adding, "If there is a God, I am glad to believe in him, all he needs to do is appear to me!" This proposition seems to appeal to a certain group of atheists and agnostics, while other atheists and agnostics do not subscribe to it.

I have tried to carefully consider this argument and readily state I do not find this persuasive. It is premised, at least in part, on the idea that God would behave as I would if I were God. Of course, I am no God, and it seems a bit narcissistic to think that God should or would be what I want him to be. I can't even make people be what or who I want them to be!

This perspective seems to have taken the biblical story of creation and turned it on its head. Instead of God making humanity in his image, this is humanity trying to make a God in our image. If God is not a visible being, then God is not a visible being.

The Judeo-Christian God stands out as different from the other neighboring religions of the day. The other perceived gods of ancient times were somewhat visible. In the Greek world, you would find

Poseidon in the ocean. The Vikings found Thor in the thunder. Israel's neighbors in Mesopotamia found Ba'al in storms. The Egyptians found Ra in the sun. The ancient people were also able to make images of their gods, and many of these "idols" can be seen in museums and are still being found by archaeologists today.

Not so Israel. The Judeo-Christian Scriptures uniquely note that God is not a visible God. Humanity has no concept of what God "looks like" and was prohibited from making any image of God. To Israel and Moses, people who had spent four hundred years living in Egypt, where hundreds of gods were painted, carved, and modeled, this must have seemed the most bizarre of the Ten Commandments.

Recorded in Exodus 20:3-4, God's clear instruction was, "You shall have no other gods before me. You shall not make for yourself a carved image, or any likeness of anything that is in heaven above, or that is in the earth beneath, or that is in the water under the earth."

This was out of place with every other culture around Israel. It did not even occur *to Moses* that God was one who couldn't be seen. After God had led the Israelites out from Pharaoh's control, while Moses was on the mountain receiving God's instructions for the people, Moses asked God to show himself. Moses wanted to see God.

God told Moses that Moses would see God's glory. Moses would see where God had been, but Moses could not see God's face. God explained, "You cannot see my face, for man shall not see me and live" (Ex. 33:20).

While this was unlike any other contemporary religion, this revelation about God makes sense considering what is known about the universe today. At the time I write this, most scholars believe that there are 100,000,000,000,000,000,000,000 (100 sextillion, or 10^{23}) stars in the universe. Like earth's sun, each of those stars has their own gravitational pull with their own cosmic bodies captured in the field. If I could travel in the universe at the speed of light, it would take 93 billion years to go from one end to the other. The Judeo-Christian Scriptures teach that those stars are each named by God (Ps 147:4), and

God spread the whole universe with his hand (Is 48:13). This same God knows the thoughts of each of the eight billion people alive today.

God is so great and grand that many reading this description would find such a God inconceivable. He is much too large for the human mind to even conceive. His power, insight, and role in this world seem too great for even the smartest of a human's three-pound brain.

Yet it is exactly that reality that makes it sensible that such a God isn't going to be seen by you and me. God isn't Thor walking in the thunder and occasionally displaying his hammering in the storms that rock the land and sea. God is far more than a storm, a planet, a solar system, or even the universe.

The Judeo-Christian God who created this universe is far beyond what any eye could behold. To some, it seems almost ludicrous to think that one could see God, much less that such a God would make personal visits to the eight billion people on the planet, answering their questions, and convincing them he really is such a God. Yet to others who believe God does have a personal interest in all eight billion people, seeking a unique relationship with each one, it isn't ludicrous. These recognize the truth, however, that God is so much more than could be taken in by immediate human physical perception.

Importantly, however, here is one of the dynamics of the Christian faith. Christianity teaches that such an unfathomable God did, in a sense, become visible once for all mankind to see and know. The Christian teaching is that God miraculously became incarnated into a human form in the person of Jesus. Christian orthodoxy teaches that Jesus was fully God and fully human.

I find the idea of an incarnation easy to accept. Similarly, the idea that it would happen in a miraculous fashion (a virgin birth) is not out of the question. In fact, something extraordinary would almost be expected, if there were such a God doing such a thing as becoming human. What I would find nonsensical, or at least hard to expect, is that any such huge God as taught in the Judeo-Christian Scriptures could appear in his true state as a human.

The amazing thing about the Christian explanation is timing. In its earliest writings, the Bible sets aside such concerns of seeing God, even though the concerns haven't really come into mind until the explosion of knowledge post-Renaissance. In a way that would seem "too convenient" as an explanation if it came today, the underlying issues of physically seeing God were dealt with in Christian Scriptures long ago. It involves not only God's explanation to Moses I reference above but also a discussion of what it means for Jesus to be "fully God."

The Christian Scriptures teach that Jesus was God's Son and was the divine one. But Scripture also teaches that in becoming human, God set aside aspects of his "God-ness." The Jewish lawyer and Christian apostle Paul wrote about this to a group of Christians in Philippi (modern Greece). Paul explained that Jesus, "though he was in the form of God, did not count equality with God a thing to be grasped, but emptied himself, by taking the form of a servant, being born in the likeness of men" (Phil 2:6-7).

Even Jesus explained to his followers that, powerful as he was, there were things even he did not know. When speaking of the end of days, Jesus noted that such knowledge was possessed by God alone, not angels nor himself as Jesus Christ, Son of God (Mt 24:36).

As one might suspect, God becoming man, even "emptying himself" did not mean that Jesus was any ordinary human. The Christian Scriptures proclaim that Jesus did great miracles, healing the sick, raising the dead, multiplying fish and bread to feed thousands, changing water into wine, and more. These miracles are not anything I can see or verify today. But in their day, they were strong enough to convince so many people that within two decades of the life of Christ, belief in him as the Son of God had spread throughout much of the Roman world. Ultimately many, including the closest followers of Jesus, would die as martyrs rather than recant their confidence in who he was and what he did.

So as I consider the God proclaimed in the Bible, and as I consider what kind of God it would take to be over all the universe, I don't find it bizarre that I don't see him in a physical form. God is beyond this universe and its physical features. I am not shocked I don't see him. My shock is that such a grand God would care for people, or even pay anyone any attention. I am not alone in this amazement. The writer of Psalm 8 was also stunned, exclaiming, "O LORD, our Lord, how majestic is your name in all the earth! You have set your glory above the heavens. When I look at your heavens, the work of your fingers, the moon and the stars, which you have set in place, what is man that you are mindful of him, and the son of man that you care for him?" (Ps 8:1, 3, 4).

This is the thrust of Jesus as God incarnate. Humanity has a visible incarnation of God that was so powerful, compelling, and genuine that people readily gave their lives rather than deny the veracity of what they saw and experienced. This is especially true concerning the resurrection of Jesus from the dead, the ultimate proof that he was God, not simply a good guy. Jesus did this, as per his teaching and that of his followers, because of his love and concern for humanity. God cares for people because he made humanity in his image to be in a relationship with him. He then worked to restore the relationship destroyed by sin.

To me, the visibility issue is not one that weighs in favor of "No God." It is consistent with the views of the Judeo-Christian God.

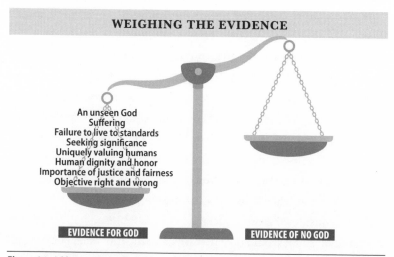

Figure 9.1. Adding an unseen God

WHY DO SO MANY PRAYERS SEEM UNANSWERED?

A third argument often given as proof against God centers on prayer. If there is a God, and if he cares for humanity, why is it so many prayers of people go unanswered? Of course, one might excuse the unanswered prayer of the child who prays for an immediate ice cream cone, or maybe for the blizzard to cancel school. But what about the victim of inoperable cancer? What about the child who prays to God that she not be molested again? Why doesn't God always answer those prayers, "Yes"?

When I was a young boy, age eleven, I was going to bed on a Friday night, getting up early the next morning for a baseball game. It was an important game for our team and was played in a big field, complete with a scoreboard just over the centerfield fence. I prayed that night that I would hit a home run the next day. Sure enough, in my first at bat, I hit one that sailed clear over the center field fence.

Look at the possibilities: Did God answer that prayer? Or did I get lucky? Maybe my prayer had infiltrated my subconscious mind and even though there is no God, I had the confidence to swing mightily and accurately. In faith, I can say, "God answered my prayer," but to use that as a basis for faith seems tenuous at best. Similarly, there were times I prayed to hit a home run, and I struck out. Did God answer the prayer, "No!"? Or was I unlucky? Did my prayer not adequately infuse my subconscious mind such that I was successful? Again, this seems tenuous to use prayer for any argument for or against God.

Take this example to another scale. After a college football game, I was listening to the post-game show on the radio. One of the players from the victorious team was explaining, "I knew we would win. We prayed to win." I can safely assume that both sides had players, coaches, or at least fans praying that each side would win. How can one fairly build a faith, or a lack of faith, based upon those results? I don't think anyone can.

I can better answer the question, "If there is a God, why are so many prayers unanswered?" by looking at this practically. There are certain prior questions that need answers, and structuring a discussion around those questions helps me make sense of this issue: What is the purpose of prayer? How should people pray? Are there limits to prayer?

WHAT IS THE PURPOSE OF PRAYER?

The purpose from a human perspective might be as simple as, "I want something that I can't get on my own." The purpose from God's perspective might be something different.

If I know much of humanity, I know that the human tendency is to make the world about us. *We* want what *we* want. *Our* needs are important. *Our* priorities matter. Yet that inherent narcissism does not necessarily reflect reality. The Judeo-Christian view of reality is quite different. The big concern is not, "Am I going to be happy today?" There are much bigger concerns.

The Judeo-Christian teaching is that people live in a war zone. There is a cosmic conflict in which people play a role. God has put humanity on this earth with the plan that, working in concert and relationship with God, humanity should "tend to the garden," taking care of each other and this planet, and earnestly seek God's kingdom. This should affect how I treat people, animals, and the environment.

Since the fall of Adam and Eve, humanity is at greater odds for overcoming in the conflicts of this world and life. A paramount issue becomes restoring the relationship with God, something made possible through the actions of God in Jesus. This can bring people back into relationship with God, and it infuses people with heightened insight and power to do certain things, but it doesn't suddenly make the world and my mission one of happiness to the greatest number of people.

The Christian teaching is that those who follow God are to live their lives seeking what will best promote God's kingdom, best ensure that things bring glory to his name, and best fight against the foes that are set against him. That might mean healing of my cancer will help. It might also mean that a cancer leading to my death would help. I don't know. I am not God. But Christian prayer in this life is not about my will, it's not about my comfort or feelings, it's not about me or you. Christian prayer is about God's will. Jesus taught his disciples to pray, "Thy will be done on earth as it is in heaven" (Mt 6:10).

Under Christian thought, does God's will not take into account how I feel? Of course it does. God cares for his followers as a good parent does his or her child. But there are matters that are of greater importance in life than how I feel. My parents were marvelous parents. As I grew up, there were times when I got the bicycle I wanted. But there were also times when I didn't get what I wanted. There were times my feelings were trumped by greater needs, sometimes even my own needs to grow up, to learn responsibility, and to do what needed to be done, whether I wanted to or not.

Under Christian teaching, so it is with God. Prayers are important, but prayers fill a role. People should be seeking God's will in this world and praying that into reality. In an allegorical way, people are "tending to the garden," but praying for God's help in doing so.

HOW SHOULD I PRAY?

It makes sense that I should not be indicting God over not answering unanswered prayers unless I am certain that I am praying as I should. Certainly, the purpose of prayer must inform me in how I should pray.

Jesus taught his followers a good deal about prayer. He told his followers to pray together. He told them their prayers would be answered. But he told them this in conjunction with teaching them *how to pray*. Here the "how" becomes extremely important.

One time after Jesus had finished praying, his followers came up to him and asked him, "Lord, teach us to pray" (Lk 11:1). Jesus did so. The more common version of Jesus teaching prayer is recorded in Matthew 6. It is called the Lord's Prayer, and it teaches how the believer is to pray: "Our Father in heaven, hallowed be your name. Your kingdom come, your will be done, on earth as it is in heaven. Give us this day our daily bread, and forgive us our debts, as we also have forgiven our debtors. And lead us not into temptation, but deliver us from evil."

That prayer is vastly different from "Give me a bicycle!" One sees in Jesus's prayer that the greater matter is not about me. The first thing in the prayer is for God's name to be "hallowed." The idea behind "name" is reputation. The "hallowing" means holding it in regard, seeing it as special and unique. I am to pray that God's reputation and essence as understood and seen in this world will be uniquely honored and valued.

From there the prayer seeks God's kingdom, not my own. I am praying for God's kingdom to expand and grow, for people to move into faith. As a Christian believer, my prayer would include that this book would assist others and bring growth to his kingdom. I write my experiences and thoughts with people in mind that may not yet embrace the truth of what I believe to be reality. My prayer is that this would happen in the mind and heart of each one reading it.

The third concern in the prayer centers on the importance of seeking God's will. I would like a number of things in my life, but the real thing I should seek is God's will. If I want to be well but through my sickness I or others will grow in faith, then let me be sick! If my death will help others find the way, if it will work better in God's kingdom for me to meet death today instead of tomorrow, then Lord, take me today!

Only after praying for God's name, God's kingdom, and God's will, did Jesus teach one to pray for one's own needs. Even those needs, however, are instructive. Jesus taught prayer for what one *needs* today. Of course, there are differences in what I need and what I want. I don't see Jesus teaching his disciples that prayer is a birthday wish list. It is for the good of God and our needs. The second personalized request is for the forgiveness of sins, but with a twist. I am also to pray and recognize my own need to forgive others. The final plea in prayer is for God to help me walk right and holy before him, delivering me from temptation and evil.

This approach to prayer is very different from one where God is a concierge getting me seats in the restaurant that is otherwise hard to get. God is no bellhop hauling my luggage to my room. God is God. This world and people's lives are serious. There is suffering, there are enemies, and sin runs rampant. I am to be praying against those things as I pray for God's will.

These are prayers God answers. This brings me to ask one final question.

ARE THERE LIMITS TO PRAYER?

If one argues for prayer to be the litmus test on whether there is a God, one must be thinking there are no limits to prayer. However, the Judeo-Christian teaching is that prayer is very limited. It is limited by God's will and by what best achieves God's purposes. Again, while humanity is very special in the Judeo-Christian worldview, people are not the be all or end all. People have a role to fill in God's creation pursuant to God's instructions and plans. So it is not surprising to see, even in the Bible, numerous times prayers are answered "no," "wait," or even, "I have a better idea."

Several examples should suffice. The apostle Paul was able to perform great miracles on the road. He healed the sick, cast out demons, and even raised the dead once. Yet there was an infirmity that afflicted Paul personally that he prayed to go away three times. The unnamed infirmity remained. Paul explained to some of his Christian friends that his "thorn in the flesh" was there at least in part to keep him from becoming "conceited" over the many accomplishments and honors he had from God. Paul's prayer to remove the thorn was not answered, but instead Paul was taught that in his weakness, he would find the strength of God (see 2 Cor 12:1-12). King David, the greatest Hebrew king, had an infant son from an adulterous relationship. The son was born terminally sick. David prayed for healing day and night. David fasted. The son died (2 Sam 12). Even Jesus himself prayed before his arrest, knowing what was coming. Jesus asked God that the ordeal might pass, praying, "Father, if you are willing, remove this cup from me," but the prayer didn't end there. Jesus then added, "Nevertheless, not my will, but yours, be done" (Lk 22:42).

The Judeo-Christian position is not one of a genie God who is required to grant one wishes. Prayer is not a magic formula that binds God to answer as one wants. Prayer is a way of aligning my desires with the will of God. Prayer invokes and works God's plans on earth so that humanity can fulfill and walk in God's will. It is not all about me or you. It is all about him.

Answering these questions about prayer help bring into focus whether or how prayer should fit into the scales of evidence on whether God exists. The idea that God doesn't answer all prayer is not indicative to me that there is no God. I would agree there is no genie, but common sense dictates that God couldn't be bound by such simple expectations. That would change sports quite a bit if God ensured victory by the team with the most prayers. I think that, as a general rule, God lets/enables things to be themselves. So he allows a game of skill to be a game of skill—not a pray-off!

I see prayer, both answered and unanswered, as consistent with the worldview of the Judeo-Christian God. It seems to me that it could also be consistent with there being no God but luck, save for the fact that occasionally a prayer is answered in a miraculous fashion. That would sway those who experience the miracle, but not the cynic. Accordingly, I leave answered or unanswered prayer off the scales for others, but I include it on the scales for myself.

10

SCIENCE
AND FAITH

THE FOURTH NEGATIVE PERCEPTION about a belief in the biblical God is so important that it deserves its own chapter. If you want to see some heated debate, begin a discussion in certain circles about the first chapter of Genesis! Creation versus evolution is guaranteed to pique most anyone's interest. But the debate doesn't stop there. Among committed Jews and Christians, you can find finer debates of how one should read the creation passages. Are they literal? Figurative? If literal, how literal? If figurative, how figurative?

My concern in my examination is the overarching question of whether science and faith conflict with each other. For me, that includes a careful examination of Genesis 1. In examining it carefully, the passage explodes with meaning that somehow can get lost in the frenzy of trying to parse precise details of a literal interpretation.

I was trying a case about a boat that capsized. In the trial, I offered the expert testimony of a man named Captain Disler. At the beginning of his testimony, I thought it important to let the jury know Captain Disler was eminently qualified. So among the questions I asked was this, "Captain Disler, have you sailed the Seven Seas?" Captain Disler then explained to the jury that the *Seven Seas* was an antiquated term with roots in the era of the Roman Empire. In today's nomenclature, there were many more than seven seas, and the better answer was that he had piloted ships in every major body of water.

Later in the case, the defense put on an expert to counter the testimony of Captain Disler. I thought that this expert was unqualified and had insufficient knowledge on the substance at issue. In my cross-examination, I asked him, "Have you sailed the Seven Seas?"

The jury knew what answer should be forthcoming, but the witness just hemmed and hawed in response. I followed up, "Can you even name the Seven Seas?"

Of course, the jury knew, as I did, that as a vestige term from two thousand years ago without literal meaning today, there could be no real answer. Yet the "expert" didn't know that. He struggled for what seemed an eternity beginning with, "Well, you have the Atlantic and Pacific." Then he backed away from that, acknowledging that they were oceans. Finally, he gave up. The jury knew the man's qualifications were not fully up to snuff!

I remember this trial as I begin my examination of the Bible and science. The trial story parallels a concern I have over others—especially atheists—telling me how I must read and understand the Bible.

This chapter becomes important to those who believe in God and Scripture, because I seek to fix what has become distorted—a Christian view of science and the cosmos. To unbelievers like Richard Dawkins, an improper reading of Genesis is important if they are going to assign a meaning to it. Dawkins and others believe that Genesis must be read as six twenty-four-hour days of creation, and as a result, they dismiss all of faith because it is inconsistent with science. I believe if their scholarship of the Genesis text were better, they would jettison this argument. It would force them to challenge the existence of God on other grounds.

DOES A BELIEF IN GOD MESH WITH SCIENCE IN MAKING SENSE OF THE COSMOS?

Both among Bible believers and Bible cynics, one can readily find people who "read the Bible literally" and who believe that the

Judeo-Christian God must be at odds with scientific proof and evidence. Many understand that science explains the world today as a result of evolution. A number of those subscribing to Judeo-Christian teaching believe that the Bible teaches a creation of the world in seven days. Some go further and point out biblical genealogies and believe that the earth is only some six thousand years old. For many there are only two choices: believe the Bible or believe in science. This is a false dichotomy.

Popular atheist Alex Rosenberg attempts to frame the debate, setting faith and science at odds in his book *The Atheist's Guide to Reality.* "An unblinking scientific worldview requires atheism. . . . The claim that religion and science don't compete is good politics. It's also confused."[1]

Surprisingly, it isn't only the atheist who views science and faith at odds. It seems a number of believers do as well. The Internal Medicine section of the *Journal of the American Medical Association* published on an original investigation of patients choosing faith over medical treatment. In-depth interviews of twenty-one doctors conducted introduced some alarming results. "Almost all of the physicians who participated in our study described situations in which patients use religious terms to explain their disagreement with medical recommendations."[2]

The three areas of greatest conflict between doctors and patients that were deemed faith-based were

- those in which religious doctrines directly conflict with medical recommendations;
- those that involve an area in which there is extensive controversy within the broader society; and
- settings of relative medical uncertainty in which patients "choose faith over medicine."

The first category included religions (notably Jehovah's Witnesses) that viewed blood transfusions or the use of any blood products as wrong. The second category centered on issues like abortion. The third category is the one most relevant to my discussion here.

In the third category, the surveyed doctors noted patients who "trust God more than they trust us." One such cancer patient refused a colonoscopy after hundreds of polyps were revealed by screening "because she and her daughter believed in the power of prayer." Other patients refused or delayed treatment for conditions, believing, "It's in God's hands." Another patient refused important tests, explaining, "I know God will provide—I don't need that test." One lady diagnosed with breast cancer declined treatment, choosing instead to simply pray on it.

The most disturbing part of this to me isn't simply placing science and faith at odds. But placing the two as opposite ends of a teeter-totter violates what I believe is the true biblical teaching and injunction that science is humanity's tool to accomplish matters like victory over cancer. If the choice is between faith and science, then I am not surprised at anyone who chooses science. But the Bible does *not* put science and faith at odds with each other, and neither do I. The Bible teaches that people can find reliability in the cosmos and that the fundamentals of science—an ordered universe, cause and effect, and so on—go hand in hand with God as revealed through Scripture. Even beyond that, however, I think it is fair to read Scripture as teaching that God *wants* humanity to pursue science. God has given humanity not only an ability to understand nature but an *instruction* to understand nature. Science is a tool God gave humanity to better the world.

In this chapter, my goal is to see where in the scales one should place the God-versus-science debate. But before I can consider placing the debate in the scales of evidence, and before I can determine how much weight to assign it, I need to understand if it is a proper debate.

Most every workday finds me involved in a lawsuit. Lawsuits have *styles*, which is a technical name used for the label or filing information of the case. The party suing is generally termed the *plaintiff*, and the party sued is the *defendant*. In the style, the plaintiff is listed followed by a "v." or "vs.," and then the defendant. So the style might read, "Smith v. Jones" or "Smith vs. Jones." The "v." and "vs." are abbreviations for "versus." If the case is "Smith v. Jones," then Smith is suing Jones, and the two are opposed to each other. If, however, Smith and Jones are on the same side, and they are both suing Williams, then they get on the same side of the "v." and it is styled, "Smith and Jones v. Williams."

As I read the Bible, the debate framed by many as "science" on one side of the "v." and "God and the Bible" on the second side of the "v." is wrongly framed. In legal terminology, I would say, "Objection, your honor, this begs the question." Before this debate can be framed as science versus the Bible and God, I must first determine whether they might be on the same side of the "v."

To assess this fairly, I need to carefully consider the claims of the Bible as they relate to science and determine whether the two are at odds. If they are, so be it. If they aren't, this entire question as it relates to the existence of God becomes moot.

The importance of context. Most anyone can read the Bible and understand its core messages and history. But when people want to get into greater depth and probe the Bible more carefully, one should begin by placing it into context. To read the Bible as a twenty-first-century novel, textbook, or dissertation is a mistake. The Bible itself is a composite of many different writings put together over thousands of years. Those writings are in different languages, each of which in their ancient forms has ceased in common usage. The writings were products first of their historical, geographical, and cultural contexts. For this reason, careful, deliberate, and academic work is involved in plumbing the fuller depths of teachings and claims made in the Bible found within its historical context.

Any consideration of what the Bible says about science is going to have to be done very carefully. It's not that science is a post-Renaissance endeavor, for Aristotle wrote on science, but the Bible is not itself a writing on science. The Bible claims to be a historical accounting of God revealing himself through interactions with historical peoples.

This means that one needs to read the Bible in its context to understand its claims. One needs to understand the language forms and expressions, including poetry forms; and one needs to put it into its cultural and historical context.

Here is an example. If I was transported back in a time machine to 1500 BC, placed in the town of Jericho in the Rift Valley near the Jordan River, and told to write explanations to some goat herders who also maintained grapevines about how genetic modifications to their vineyard could increase resistance to mold, I would be a bit hardpressed to do it. I could discuss genetic encoding and DNA splicing, but I strongly suspect their vocabulary wouldn't have words for deoxyribonucleic acid (DNA), especially since DNA was not isolated until 1869 and wasn't correctly modeled until Drs. Watson and Crick in 1953.

I face similar problems in trials. Frequently, especially in cases of mesothelioma and other asbestos diseases, a critical issue is the historical development of knowledge linking asbestos to various physical maladies. This is termed "state of the art" testimony. Asbestos has been used for centuries, but it wasn't until the early twentieth century that specialists began to understand its link to disease. Around the middle of the twentieth century, the link between asbestos and cancer became known. Then by the 1960s, scientists determined that asbestos caused mesothelioma.

This timeline makes a huge difference in reading about the usage of asbestos. What someone had as a concern in 1890 must be understood differently than the concerns n 1970 or today.

In many fields of study, historical analysis is critical to a proper understanding of historical sources. It is no different with the Bible. So with the importance of historical context—linguistically, ideologically, culturally, and more—I examine the Bible to see if its claims about God are at odds with science, or perhaps on the same side. Here, I will use two major biblical passages for examination. First, I consider the Bible's claims about creation, weighing them against scientific claims of the origin of life. Second, I fast forward fifteen hundred years from the writings in Genesis on creation to those of the Jewish lawyer Paul in the Christian writings of the New Testament for his affirmative claims about God and the cosmos.

Creation and evolution. In light of my vineyard/DNA example, consider the ramifications on the creation story in Genesis 1. The biblical story of creation seems to date back well over a thousand years before the birth of Jesus. It is a story that spoke into an ancient civilization in a long-dead language. Still, through the hard work of amazing linguists and archaeologists, people have helpful tools to understand the context of the day as well as the language of the story.

The creation story belongs to ancient Israel, who claimed it as a divine revelation speaking into their culture giving meaning and significance to who they were, to the cosmos, and to daily life. Egypt, where Israel had lived for four centuries, as well as Canaan, to which Israel was going, had creation stories. But those stories were *nothing at all* like that given to Israel through Moses. The stark theological differences between Israel and its neighbors begin in the Genesis texts.[3] Israel got a starkly different view of God, nature, and humanity. Old Testament scholar Bill Arnold writes, "The worldview expressed in Genesis 1–4 is not just *different* from its counterpart in the literature of the ancient world; it is *opposed* to it."[4]

The Bible sets the cultural and historical context of the creation account in a deliberate moment in time. At God's direction, Moses took the Israelites from Egypt to Mount Sinai in the wilderness, and while the people stayed at the mountain's base, Moses went up on the mountain to receive God's instructions and laws. The first five books of the Bible are accordingly called the books of Moses. (Although one must note that subsequent prophets to Moses had input into those writings as is evident, inter alia, by the inclusion of the death of Moses.)

I can't overemphasize this importance. Most of my trials are jury trials. In those cases, all lawyers work tirelessly to learn all we can about our jurors. The court frequently issues written questions to potential jurors. These are to ferret out personal information in the least intrusive fashion. We also have our teams scour through social media, and we routinely examine all available data to learn about our jurors. Why? Certainly, one important reason is to verify that the jurors are qualified to sit on the case.

But there is another reason that is just as important. I need to know how the jurors think. What is their knowledge base? If I am going to teach them the case, what do they already know? If my case is a simple auto collision, do my jurors know how to drive? If my case involves medical issues, are any of my jurors nurses or doctors? I tried a talc/ovarian cancer case with a juror who was a scientist for DuPont. I knew she would grasp aspects of the science much differently than a a sixty-year-old butcher who had never been on the internet.

That Moses was the recipient and genesis of these stories, including that of creation, puts a specific context front and center. After all, Moses was reared in the household of Pharaoh. Growing up there, as Stephen explained in his final discourse before his martyrdom, "Moses was instructed in all the wisdom of the Egyptians" (Acts 7:22).

What wisdom would Moses have learned? What kind of juror or audience was Moses? Moses' education would have centered on the gods of Egypt. Egyptian wisdom was bound up in its religion. Gods were the identifiers for almost every natural phenomenon. Animals were deified, the elements were seen as gods, and even Pharaoh himself was deemed a god. With gods for each household, gods for the various villages and towns, and the universal gods (the sun, the sky, etc.), every aspect of Egyptian wisdom and life was wrapped up in learning and understanding how to invoke and please the various deities. Pharaoh was responsible for keeping the divine order (or *maat*) to secure Egypt's safety from foreign invaders as well as natural disasters.

One is hard-pressed to put into a few sentences the relevant Egyptian wisdom/religious teachings likely known by Moses. Egyptian religion was shaped over millennia, and was not one, constant storyline, like that found in the Bible. Egypt's gods changed in significance, associated mythologies, and usage over thousands of years. Yet one is not without some core ideas that are fair to ascribe to Moses' rearing and state of knowledge at the time.

The Bible places Moses during what scholars call the New Kingdom period of Egypt (c. 1550–1069 BC). If the references to "Rameses" in Exodus 12:37 and similar passages indicate an exodus date in the 1200s BC, then Moses would have been reared in the house of Pharaoh Seti I, alongside Rameses II, who would have been the Pharaoh of the exodus. Seti I gives one a first-rate insight into the religion of Moses' upbringing because Seti's temple/tomb at Abydos has been remarkably preserved. Rameses II's tomb is also informative for the period.

Seti's temple was built immediately next to the Osireion, a symbolic burial place of the god Osiris. From among these sites, and others, one can garner important information about the gods taught to Moses. These gods stand in stark contrast to Israel's God revealed in the teachings of the Genesis creation texts. Core differences include the view of God, nature, and humanity. Read in context, one can readily see that God's concern with Moses was *not* fixing his science but fixing his theology! Consider these "lessons" for Moses as a proper framework for understanding Genesis.

GOD

One God versus many. The first and obvious difference in Israel's claimed revelation is the number of gods. Egypt had so many gods, scholars can't really determine a precise number. Most accord Egypt with upward of two thousand gods. The gods of Egypt had their own domains, and at times would fight over this, that, or the other. These domains and interactions would have been the bread and butter of Moses's education in Pharaoh's household.

On Sinai, God taught Moses a different theology. Rather than believing in many deities, there was only one. One God created everything: heavens, earth, sky, seas, land, vegetation, sun, moon, stars, animals, and man. There are no gods for each item or area. There is no competition between gods. There is no need. The one God as revealed is over all of nature. He controls everything.

The nineteenth-century Jewish Rabbi Samson Hirsch wrote in his commentary on Genesis that the full creation of everything by God signifies a God who "rules completely freely over the material and form of all creatures, over the forces that work in matter, over the laws that govern the working, and over the resulting forms."[5]

God is above creation, not a part of creation. Rabbi Hirsch contrasts the polytheistic neighbors of Israel who believed that there were preexisting forces in nature to which even the gods were subject. Toward that end, many gods must have existed to deal with the many aspects of nature. No one God was over nature.[6]

An extension of Hirsch's point made earlier is the transcendence of God. As a God who existed before any creation, and as the God who does the actual creating, this God is apart from the things created. In this sense, God becomes the "Super Nature," the one beyond and outside of the natural order.

In Genesis, God creates all things. One must note how different this was from Israel's neighbors. For many of the neighbors, the gods themselves *were* the sky, the moon, the sun, and so on (or at least they were inextricably linked to those elements of nature).

Egyptian papyri repeatedly show pictures that illustrate the "science" or "theology" that would have been the wisdom taught to Moses growing up in Pharaoh's house. A frequent teaching has the god Seb (a.k.a. Geb) lying out as the god of the earth. His upraised knee denotes the hills and valleys, while he has one hand raised toward the sky and another toward earth. Above Seb, in a pose somewhat akin to the "cat" pose in yoga, stretched out the goddess Nut, the wife of Seb. In some pictures Nut has stars on her body. She was the "heavens," and is frequently shown separated from Seb (the earth) by a god with upraised hands. This god is Shu, the god who was the sky. Other gods, including the sun, moon, and stars, would come forth from various parts of Nut and then return at their appropriate times.[7] In some papyri, Shu was not only holding up Nut, but with the help of another four to eight gods, Shu also held back the waters in the heavens.

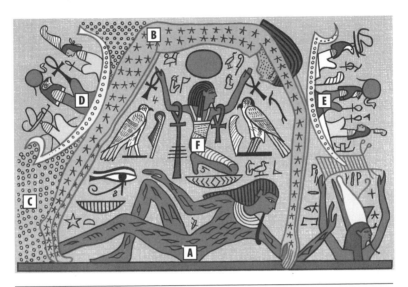

Figure 10.1. In this view of the world, the earth is the god Seb (figure A), who lies in a way that creates hills and valleys. Above him is the sky goddess Nut (figure B). Affixed to her are the stars. She holds back the waters in the heavens, represented by tiny circles or raindrops (figure C). The sun god Ra, wearing the sun disk on his head, rides the back of Nut in a boat on the heavenly waters rising in the morning and setting in the evening (figures D and E). The goddess Shu (figure F) is the air, helping to hold up Nut (the sky).

Not so with God as revealed to Israel. He was not found in the earth, sky, or sun; God made the earth, sky, and sun. God was beyond creation and controlled creation. This merges into the next difference.

God is outside space/time, not captive to space/time. When speaking of space and time, I am using modern scientific ideas and words. However, the gist of those concepts are valid ways to verbalize a difference in understanding what came from Israel's revelation distinct from the imaginings of her neighbors.

A singular God who reigns over all nature, whether in space or time, is a God who is not subject to the laws of nature. This is a miracle-working God who can bend, suspend, or alter things at the mere word of his mouth. An over-age couple can have a baby, dreams can have meaning, famines can be foreseen, bushes can burn without getting burned up, seas can be parted, and people can be delivered— all of which one reads in the books of Moses.

In contrast, Egyptian mythology taught that the self-created god Ra made the winds, water, and world by creating more gods. Ra placed the goddess Nut above the earth, and the goddess *was* the sky, wearing a blue dress. As Nut became weary from holding up the stars, planets, and even Ra (the sun), Ra ordered the god of air (Shu) to stand on the earth and support the heavenly Nut. Shu couldn't do this without standing on Geb, the god who *was* the earth. Ra was captive to the cycle of traversing the sky each day. To help brighten the night, Ra made the moon and entrusted it to another god (Thoth).

In his daily trek across the sky (Nut), Ra brought light and warmth to the world, but at night he had to travel the length of the world below before he could rise again on the other side. Each night Ra was threatened by Apophia, a monstrous serpent, and his fiendish minions. As certain as the dawn, however, Ra defeated this nightly assault.

The cultures north of Egypt also had the gods captive to space and time. In the *Enuma Elish*, a Mesopotamian creation story, the main god (Apsu) is put to sleep by a magic spell cast by his offspring, a god named Ea. While asleep, Apsu is tied up and killed.[8] This can happen when gods are not over the laws of nature (or its magical spells, as those laws were deemed to include in that era). Israel's revelation showed that God was not so vulnerable. God was above creation, neither a part of it nor subject to it.

Another aspect of God's existence beyond space and time is the genesis of God himself. Over and over in the writings of Israel's neighbors, one reads ideas and stories of how the gods were made. In the *Enuma Elish*, Apsu and Tiamat "were mingling their waters together" when "the gods were formed between them." In commenting upon it, translator Benjamin Foster adds: "This elaborate theogony [creation of gods], or genealogy of the gods, builds on Sumerian precedent. It finds a parallel in Hesiod's version of Greek mythology, and is perhaps its ultimate source, but is absent in the Bible."[9]

Not so for the true God revealed to Moses and Israel. God explained himself as beyond the material world and its time. God *made* time (morning and evening, day one, etc.); he was not subject to time. Scripture would later reveal that God's eternal nature included no beginning and no end.

An important distinction between gods who are wrapped up in nature, and Israel's God who revealed himself as beyond nature, arises in the area of science. If, as Israel's neighbors believed, capricious gods *are* the storms, then one tries to determine or secure good weather by appeasing the gods. Israel was taught, however, that God made the world and wasn't found in the world. The world was orderly and to be understood. This understanding opened the door for science over magic.[10]

God is not a sexual being. As Israel's neighbors went about constructing images of the gods, they conceived of the gods as they did all other beings—male and female. Not like the unique view Israel got from revelation.

A reading of the Hittite legends includes sordid tales of physical and sexual conquest among the gods that impact their interactions with creation. In *Elkunirsa and Asertu*, one reads of the god El (creator of earth) and his goddess wife Asertu. Without El's knowledge, Asertu attempts to seduce the god Ba'al, who refuses her advances. Asertu then complains to her husband and we read about the gods plotting and scheming behind each one's back in a divine saga that reads like a lurid soap opera.[11]

This is typical of humanity's construction of gods in people's image rather than a revelation of God beyond human thought. Genesis is careful to teach that God made people in his image, both male and female (Gen 1:27). As such, God is neither male nor female, but both sexes find themselves expressing some aspects of God.

God does not have human limitations. Israel's God is not a person in a super-sized form. God does not have human limitations of strength, drive, or emotions. This sets apart the gods as imagined by Israel's neighbors.

Contrast the gods in the *Enuma Elish*. A point was reached where the younger gods were bothersome to the older gods because of their "offensive behavior" and their "noisome actions." The older god Apsu yelled at his wife (mother of the younger gods): "Their behavior is noisome to me! By day I have no rest, at night I do not sleep! I wish to put an end to their behavior, to do away with it! Let silence reign that we may sleep!"[12] With that, the gods started plotting to kill each other. After the killing starts, war rages for some time until a peaceful accord is reached.

As one continues to read the story, one sees more human limitations on the gods. One principal victor in the *Enuma Elish* was the god Marduk. Marduk was also the god who made the decision to create people. His reason? The gods were tired from their hard work! People were made to "bear the gods' burden that those [the gods] may rest."[13]

Similarly, in the Atrahasis, people were made because of divine exhaustion: "did forced labor . . . digging watercourses . . . They heaped up all the mountains. . . . Forced labor they bore night and day. [They were com]plaining, denouncing, [mut]tering down in the ditch. . . . [The gods then say], 'Let the midwife create a human being, let man assume the drudgery of god.'"[14]

The gods were also subject to human pouting. In a Hittite story, one god named Telipinu gets angry, leaves his job post, and goes to sleep in a meadow. This was ultra-important to the ancient people. Consider: "In the Hittite view, the operation of the universe required that each deity and human conscientiously perform his or her proper function within the whole. Calamity manifested in some sector of the cosmos was an indication that the god or goddess responsible for it had become angry and had abandoned his or her post."[15]

Once Telipinu leaves, the world falls apart. Breeding of livestock stopped, the weather went haywire, crops would not grow as famine hit the land, and even the gods themselves could not eat a satisfying meal. The Storm-god (Telipinu's father) does not know where his son is and refuses to go look for him despite his wife's (the "Mother-goddess") vehement demands. So the Mother-goddess sends a bee to find her son, the god Telipinu.

The bee finds the god, stings him a few times to wake him up, which only increases his anger. At that point, everyone (human and divine) went to work to get Telipinu in a better mood and restore order to the world!

Into these cultures and these mindsets comes Israel's unique revelation of God as Creator given in Genesis. God is not a larger version of a human. He has none of the human foibles. In fact, humanity itself has none of those foibles until sin enters the picture.

Creation was not hard work for God. He spoke and it came to be, over and over again. At the end of six days of creation, there was a day of rest, but the text gives no indication that God was tired, and hence resting on the seventh day. Instead, the "rest" of the Sabbath was at its core the simple "stopping" of the creative activity.

Sabbath is the anglicized version of the Hebrew word formed from the root *sbt*. The verb in its root means "to cease."[16] On the seventh day, God quit working, but not out of fatigue. God had made a world that was very good. He quit because his work was finished. I might equate it to a rest in a musical score. The musicians are not stopping because they are tired. It is a time when the music is not to be played.

On a similar note of tiresome work, the gods in neighboring cultures had a lot of work in making humans. They had to kill gods for the necessary blood to mix with clay.[17] Needless to say, the process of figuring out which god to kill and then killing that god was no simple matter! In Genesis, one reads the contrast of God simply speaking and things coming to be. Humanity was fashioned out of the dust of the field, but no gods died for animation. God simply breathed life into man.

A final note hearkens back to Moses' learning of Egyptian wisdom. While Egyptian theology believed the serpent Apopsis lay in wait to kill the sun god Ra each night, in Genesis, Moses learned differently. The serpent tempted Adam and Eve, not God. It is unfathomable that anything could destroy or threaten God. God vanquishes the serpent, cursing him and promising to bring about his ultimate destruction through the offspring of woman. In the end, the Genesis serpent is permanently defeated.

NATURE

I was involved in litigation involving a Japanese car that had "unintended acceleration." It wasn't my first case where many witnesses spoke a foreign language, and where documents were in a foreign language. I had to have translators. In depositions, the translators would listen to my question in English and ask it in Japanese, the witness would answer in Japanese, and the translator would put the answer into English.

The court reporter was responsible for taking all the testimony, but the court reporter could report only the English. The Japanese was never taken down. In a few cases, the testimony was so critical that we had two translators, a second running a check to make sure the first one didn't make an error.

Those cases are always more difficult to handle, and misunderstandings readily occur. The language is not the only barrier; the cultural distinctions are barriers too. Company allegiance means something different in different cultures. Even something as simple as a bow or handshake denotes something different. In cases where Russian witnesses have testified, smiling is not the cultural norm among most Russians, while it is in certain parts of America. That doesn't mean the Russians are less honest or even less friendly. It is simply a cultural distinction.

These legal experiences weigh heavily on my analysis of the Genesis creation story. I approach this with a full and fair recognition that I am not only dealing with language differences, the ancient Hebrew being put into modern English, but I am also dealing with massive cultural differences. The creation story recounts something from a culture thousands of years ago in a faraway part of the world.

Before someone blindly accuses the creation story of being at odds with science, one needs to understand the creation story in its full context. That means not only translating the ancient Hebrew into modern English, but also placing it into its ancient culture to first understand what it meant to its original recipients. When one does so, the idea that the creation story conflicts with science and nature is shown to be illusory.

As one considers what Genesis says about nature, it helps to distinguish between *cosmology* and *function*. Cosmology refers to the way the ancients understood the universe. One might call it their language of the cosmos. In contrast, my cosmology is one of the universe as a vacuum where solar systems occupy space, where stars are distant suns, and where the planets rotate around those suns. I think of Earth as round, surrounded by an atmosphere. Clouds are a gathering of condensation and moisture. Mountains are areas where Earth has projected up from the planet. The seas are the waters that have accumulated in low-lying areas. The tides are a gravitational response to the moon. This is my language of Earth, and I can write, speak, and communicate with these terms and ideas.

Israel and its neighbors did not speak my language of cosmology. Of course, God's revelation uses terms that would have made sense to the Israelites, even though they are at odds with the terms of understanding today. This is the importance of context in language as well as culture and ideas.

Ancient Near Eastern scholar John Walton makes the point: "If we aspire to understand the culture and literature of the ancient world, whether Canaanite, Babylonian, Egyptian, or Israelite, it is essential that we understand their cosmic geography. Despite variations from one ancient Near Eastern culture to another, there are certain elements that characterize all of them."[18]

I like the ancient cosmology, not because it is accurate, but because it makes sense how an observant person would have understood it. The ancients thought of the cosmos as layers, much like a three-layer cake. The earth was the middle layer. The heavens were the top layer, and the netherworld was the bottom (literally the "underworld"). The people did not think of multiple continents but thought of one stretch of land that was shaped like a disc. At the edges of this disk were mountains that held up the sky. It's as if the sky was the frosting between the top two layers with the heavens (layer three) being above the sky.

Figure 10.2. In this view of the heavens, the firmament (the long bar at figure A) holds back the heavenly waters (the wavy lines at figure B). Affixed to the top of the firmament are the stars (the circles partially on the firmament at figure A, and partially in the waters at figure B). The sun god Shamash (figure C) sits enthroned above with his radiant sun (figure D).

The sun moved across the sky during the day and returned through the underworld at night to begin its journey again the next morning.[19] Stars were on tracks that set their course and they would come out at night and move on course. The earth itself floated on waters, which were kept from overcoming the earth by the force of the sky. There were also waters above the sky which, when the windows of heaven were opened, fell through the sky to the ground (see fig. 10.3).

This language is used in Genesis as the creation teaches its unique lessons of function. So, for example, Genesis 1:6-8 reads: "And God said, 'Let there be an expanse in the midst of the waters, and let it separate the waters from the waters.' And God made the expanse and separated the waters that were under the expanse from the waters that were above the expanse. And it was so. And God called the expanse Heaven."

This language is speaking God's function into the cosmos language of the Israelites. Similarly, the following verses gather the lower waters together into one place so that dry land appeared (Gen 1:9-10). God also filled the expanse of heaven with the sun, moon, and stars (Gen 1:14-18). This language of the cosmos is also used when Genesis 7:11 and 8:2 speak of the windows of heaven opening, bringing rain, and closing, stopping the rain.

Where the Genesis creation account stands out from the secular versions is in the makeup and the function of this cosmic geography. For most of Israel's neighbors, these celestial features were associated with individual gods. To Israel was revealed the truth that creation was simply that—creation. God was not the elements; God made the elements. This is true regardless of the geographical language one speaks.

Even beyond that, there is uniqueness to the function of the created cosmic elements. For Israel's neighbors, the cosmos contained elements tamed by the gods and then used for the gods' purposes. Humanity was made to work the cosmos to the benefit of the gods. Genesis sets the story the other way around.

In Genesis, God makes the cosmos for people. God sets the forms of heaven, earth, sky, and seas, filling them with fish, birds, and animals. Each is set to produce more after its own kind. These are made with the

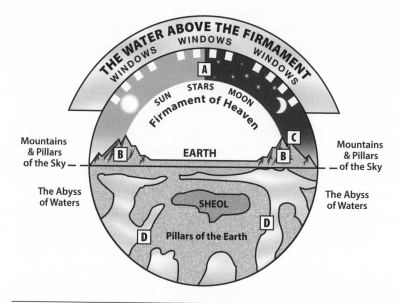

Figure 10.3. The ancients based their understanding of the world on observation and experience. They knew from rain that there must be water in the heavens. That water would fall constantly if there wasn't something holding it back. That "something" was the firmament. The rain came from clouds, so the clouds were, in effect, windows that opened in the firmament to let some of the water fall to earth. The firmament needed to be held up, so some cultures thought the far distant mountains help up the firmament. Others thought it more likely massive tent poles. The ancients knew there was water surrounding land (the seas and oceans, as well as water under the land evidenced by wells, lakes, and springs). Because land should sink in the presence of water, the land had to have some support, hence the ancients believed that foundations supported the earth/land. It amazed the ancients that the water was kept from encroaching on the land.

Even John Calvin (1509-1564) fell prey to reading Genesis for science in sixteenth-century language instead of understanding it in the vernacular of its age. Calvin thought the earth was a flat disc and saw the collection of waters away from the land and to be a miracle of God. In his commentary on Genesis, for Gen. 1:9 ("Let the waters . . . be gathered together"), Calvin wrote: "This also is an illustrious miracle, that the waters by their departure have given a dwelling-place to men. For even philosophers allow that the natural position of the waters was to cover the whole earth, as Moses declares they did in the beginning; first, because being an element, it must be circular, and because this element is heavier than the air, and lighter than the earth, it ought cover the latter in its whole circumference. But that the seas, being gathered together as on heaps, should give place for man, is seemingly preternatural; and therefore Scripture often extols the goodness of God in this particular."

As to his flat earth view, Calvin preached, "We will see some who are so deranged, not only in religion but who in all things reveal their monstrous nature, that they will say that the sun does not move, and that it is the earth which shifts and turns. When we see such minds we must indeed confess that the devil possesses them, and that God sets them before us as mirrors, in order to keep us in his fear" (John Calvin, *Opera Selecta, Corpus Refomatorum*, vol. 49, 677).

view that people would have stewardship and dominion over them, and they would serve people, not God (Gen 1:26). God makes plants as food for beasts, but ultimately for people (Gen 1:29). God sets the sun and stars but does so not for his purposes, but to set out seasons for people (Gen 1:14).

South African scholar Izak Cornelius discussed and compared ancient Near Eastern visual representations of the world with the concepts in the Old Testament in a 1994 issue of the *Journal for Northwest Semitic Languages*, concluding:

> The ancient Near Eastern mentality perceived phenomena such as the sea, heaven and sun not as natural entities, but as numinous powers. The idea of the tripartite world (heaven, earth and underworld or subterrestrial water) persists in all ancient Near Eastern cultures. The Hebrew Bible contains some of these ideas, e.g., the winged sun, the pillars of the earth and the chaotic ocean, but gave an *interpretatio Israelitica* [an interpretation unique to Israel] to them. YHWH is the one who created with wisdom and controls the powers of nature.[20]

Cornelius points out that in the Scriptures, heaven and the primeval waters are not divine powers but simply God's creation. In Scripture, God upholds the pillars of the earth; God exercises dominion over the stars, the sun, and even the underworld, and it was God who established the world through wisdom. ("The Lord by wisdom founded the earth; by understanding he established the heavens" [Prov 3:19].)

HUMANITY

Like the conception of God, the creation story's recounting of man/ woman and their purpose and role is as different from that of Israel's neighbors as night is from day. Only Genesis speaks clearly of two people as the progenitors of the entire human race; the neighbors have the gods making people in groups.[21] Also unlike Genesis, multiple ancient Near Eastern (ANE) accounts have the creating deities providing necessary physical elements in making humans (tears, flesh, blood, etc.) often mixed with clay. This shows the connection between humans and deities by shared physical material. In Genesis, however, the connection is by the breath (Spirit) that God provides to people as God makes people in his image. This sets people in a connection that is a familiar relationship with the Creator (walking and talking in the Garden of Eden), not simply some lesser extension.

Genesis does say that people were made in God's "image" (Gen. 1:26-27). Walton notes that in the ANE, it was usually the king who represented the image of God, not everyone else. Image was not physical likeness but rather a responsibility and identity of role and function.[22] In other words, people had the responsibilities God assigned as well as the abilities necessary to accomplish the tasks. Scholars have recognized various inherent ways God made people in his image in this sense.

Humanity can create, think, choose, plan, accomplish, appreciate, discern, process, and communicate. These abilities are those that God possesses and dispensed to everyone. In the revelation of Scripture, humans are embodied with the necessary qualities of God to do his work as his representatives and on his behalf. The rest of Scripture will teach that humanity fell from this created state, but with the presence of the Holy Spirit and through prayer, mankind still works to fulfill the will of God on earth.

One net result of this teaching on people is the recognition that people were made for a purpose. Like creation in general, no one is an accident. No new human life—yours, mine, your spouse, your friend, or for that matter your enemy—is an accident. Creation is God's choice. People exist because God chose to put each person here.

The implications for human value are paramount. A person's value lies in the imprint of God's image. One's value is not in looks, brains, social position, physical dexterity, or athletic talent. One's value is in her and his nature as an image bearer of almighty creator God.

While this unique teaching of the Bible stands out, it leads to my ultimate question: How does this interplay with evolution? But before that, let me speak of the writings of Paul.

WHAT DOES PAUL SAY ABOUT GOD AND SCIENCE?

First a point of clarity: the Bible doesn't use the modern word *science*, but the idea of science is there nonetheless. The apostle Paul, a man trained in Jerusalem's top Jewish law and rabbinical school, accepted that Jesus Christ was the resurrected Lord after an encounter on the road from Jerusalem to Damascus. Subsequently, he became a Christian missionary and apostle to the infant church. In his ministry, Paul wrote several letters setting out core tenets of faith and practice. Perhaps none is as well studied as his letter to the church at Rome. In that letter, Paul makes a most astonishing claim about God and science. In speaking of people who deny God and his truth, Paul wrote, "For what can be known about God is plain to them, because God has shown it to them. For his invisible attributes, namely, his eternal power and divine nature, have been clearly perceived, ever since the creation of the world, in the things that have been made" (Rom 1:19-20).

This is an astonishing claim. Paul is claiming that God's "invisible attributes," especially his "divine nature," are "clearly perceived" in what scholars term the *natural world*.[23]

Paul made a claim about God and science that is worthy of inspection. Rather than conflict with science, Paul's claim about God makes sense of the cosmos in ways that tie into the reality of life I experience day by day. In several places, it is apparent what Paul thinks are God's "invisible attributes" and "divine nature." I briefly consider several of the more prominent ones.

God is a cause-and-effect God. I see this in several of Paul's writings, including the immediate context of the Romans passage set out above. In the following Romans verses, Paul continued to write,

Although they knew God, they did not honor him as God or give thanks to him, but they became futile in their thinking, and their foolish hearts were darkened. Claiming to be wise, they became fools, and exchanged the glory of the immortal God for images resembling mortal man and birds and animals and creeping things. Therefore God gave them up in the lusts of their hearts to impurity, to the dishonoring of their bodies among themselves, because they exchanged the truth about God for a lie and worshiped and served the creature rather than the Creator, who is blessed forever! Amen. (Rom 1:22-25)

This is cause and effect in its most basic form. It is cause and effect on a human level ("Although they knew . . . they did not honor . . . but became futile in their thoughts"). It is also cause and effect on a divine level ("They exchanged the glory of the immortal God for images. . . . Therefore, God gave them up in the lusts of their hearts"). This same thought of Paul tying the cause and effect of behavior to the character and nature of God is in his letter to the Galatian churches. "Do not be deceived: God is not mocked, for whatever one sows, that will he also reap. For the one who sows to his own flesh will from the flesh reap corruption, but the one who sows to the Spirit will from the Spirit reap eternal life" (Gal 6:7-8).

The idea that you reap what you sow is simply another way to say "cause and effect." Paul uses it in reference to God's nature by setting forth the premise that anything else would be a mockery of God. Science is based on cause and effect. Scientific laws include the idea that for every action, there is an equal and opposite reaction. Humanity lives in a cause-and-effect world from a scientific perspective, not a Harry Potter world of magic and unreliability.[24]

God is a consistent and reliable God. I also see an emphatic biblical theme that God is consistent, or unchanging. Hebrews 13:8 references Jesus as the "same yesterday and today and tomorrow." The Old Testament, which served as Paul's Scriptures, quoted God through the prophet Malachi as self-claiming, "For I the Lord do not change" (Mal 3:6).

The Psalms proclaimed that while the earth and nature will pass away, God is "the same," and his "years have no end" (Ps 102:25-27).

Because God is consistent, God is reliable. Paul often uses the word *faithful* to describe this attribute or nature of God. To his friend and delegate, Timothy, Paul wrote, "If we are faithless, he remains faithful—for he cannot deny himself" (2 Tim 2:13). Similarly, Paul wrote to the church at Corinth describing God's reliability to his followers, explaining, "God is faithful, and he will not let you be tempted beyond your ability" (1 Cor 10:13).

Paul's understanding of the cosmos is that such reliability would also be found in the world around me. I should be able to observe this, and I do. The scientific method relies upon the reproducibility of experiments. All things being equal, a sequence of events should produce the same results each time.

God is a moral God. Paul ties the faithfulness and consistency of God to his actions in writing to Titus about the "hope of eternal life, which God, who never lies, promised" (Titus 1:2). I have discussed the difficulty of science providing a measuring rod for objective morality. Yet the sciences show that humans are moral creatures. Paul explained it using terms closely akin to our computer ideas of programming.

Paul wrote of those "Gentiles" who did not have the revelation of God in Scripture, yet were similar in their core understanding of right and wrong. He explained in Romans 2:14-15, "For when Gentiles, who do not have the law, by nature do what the law requires, they are a law to themselves, even though they do not have the law. They show that the work of the law is written on their hearts, while their conscience also bears witness, and their conflicting thoughts accuse or even excuse them."

Paul's understanding of God and the cosmos is a plea for people to study nature, not run from it. Paul taught that as people understand it, then God is more easily understood (and is more reasonable). He suggests that what one today calls *science* provides insight into God.

Science is not against God; it is God's handwriting. It expresses aspects of God.

Paul never embraced the arbitrary gods of Greece or the gods of the elements of Mesopotamia (or even Norse myths, had Paul ever encountered such). Paul would have rejected all such gods in favor of the God of Israel. The Israelite God is over nature, and he created nature in ways that show his fingerprints. This invigorates me for scientific inquiry; it doesn't discourage it. Because God is a cause-and-effect God, I don't simply say, "God did it." I look for the "hows." It is not good enough to say, "I don't understand the brain, so—poof! God did it!" God would have a cause to what he did. There is a reason that the stars shine.

SO WHAT IS THE POINT OF SCIENCE?

The biblical teaching of science doesn't use the modern word *science* but the idea is clear. The Bible and its faith are not only consistent with science, but they promulgate science! I believe one of the most profound instructions regarding science is found in the Garden of Eden story of Genesis 2:15. After creating Adam, the text reads, "The LORD God took the man and put him in the garden of Eden to work it and keep it." In the Hebrew of this passage, two words are used for Adam's chore list. Adam is to "work" the garden (Hebrew *'avad*—עָבַד) and he is to "keep" the garden (Hebrew *shamar*—שָׁמַר). The word translated "work" references the manual labor involved in gardening—pruning grapevines, plowing a field, and so on. But the interesting word for science purposes is translated "keep."

The Hebrew word for "keep" can refer to keeping something or someone safe, but it has a related depth of meaning that is important here. The word is used for observing something thoughtfully. Over and over this word is used in the Hebrew to reference a watchman who stands at the gates of a city and analyzes strangers to determine whether to open the city gates, who reads the signals of far-off dust to determine if an army is invading, or even to watch the sun, moon, and stars to determine days and seasons.

Consider the usage of the same word in the following passages. I will italicize the word used for the Hebrew "keep" (*shamar*):

- Do you know when the mountain goats give birth? Do you *observe* the calving of the does? (Job 39:11)

- If you, O Lord, should *mark* iniquities, O Lord, who could stand? (Ps 130:3)

- He sees many things, but does not *observe* them; his ears are open, but he does not hear. (Is 42:20)

- So, it was annulled on that day, and the sheep traders, who were *watching* me, knew that it was the word of the Lord. (Zech 11:11)

When considering the broad semantic range of the Hebrew word translated "keep," one can readily see what God was instructing humanity through Adam: take responsibility for nature. *Watch* nature intelligently and attentively, and then tend to it!

When God told Adam to "keep" the garden, God wasn't instructing Adam to keep the garden safe from space invaders or even weeds. God was telling Adam to do science! Adam was to observe nature, form hypotheses, test those, and draw reasonable conclusions that would inform his work. (This is the common definition given for the scientific method, as it is known in twenty-first-century language.)

This science became even more important once humanity became sinful and was ejected from Paradise. With sin came death. It began manifesting itself in curses set out in Genesis 3. "To the woman he said, ... 'In pain you shall bring forth children.' ... And to Adam he said, ... 'Cursed is the ground because of you; in pain you shall eat of it all the days of your life; thorns and thistles it shall bring forth for you. ... By the sweat of your face you shall eat bread, till you return to the ground'" (Gen. 3:16-19).

Amid these curses, sin, disease, pain, difficulty, and more, God has given the gift of science as a tool. Science can help combat the ravages of sin. Working the fields is more productive because of science (as well as easier). With science, one can alleviate some of the pains of childbirth. With science, one can screen for cancer. Science leads to treatments for disease and greater longevity.

Science allows humanity to join in God's work to bring good from evil. Regrettably, science can also be used as a tool to further pain and anguish, but that is not God's purpose. Humanity has been given a sensible world with consistent cause and effect that is ready for scrutiny and work. Science isn't against biblical faith. Science is an expression of a working biblical faith. I put science in the scales as evidence for God, not against God.

11

EVOLUTION

A COMMON OCCURRENCE IN MY CASES happens when one begins to dig into the witnesses used for a trial. Those witnesses surprise you! They surprise you with what they think and what they say.

I was trying a case that centered on whether a brand of baby powder made with talc had asbestos in it, and whether that asbestos had caused the ovarian cancer of the plaintiffs. The defense was that the talc was asbestos free and that the women's ovarian cancer had to come from some other cause.

The defense put on the stand a medical doctor from within the company that made the baby powder. The doctor testified that as the medical director over the product she was confident that the product was safe and couldn't cause ovarian cancer. The doctor substantiated her testimony by telling the jury that her own mother had used baby powder all her life, that the baby powder was always seen at her mother's home, and that the doctor never would have let that pass, if the baby powder could cause ovarian cancer.

When the time came for me to cross-examine the doctor, I delved into the subject of her mother's usage of the baby powder. While I didn't know the answer to my questions (the adage that lawyers should never ask questions without knowing the answer is *not* an adage with which I agree!), I probed gently but firmly.

I reiterated the testimony to make sure it was fresh in everyone's mind. I then said, "I hope your mother's doing okay," hoping to make the point that just because the mother hadn't gotten sick didn't mean that it wouldn't happen one day.

The doctor responded that her mother had passed away a few years before. I said, "I'm sorry!" Then after a pause, I asked, "I don't mean to be rude, but can you tell us what she died from?"

The doctor answered quietly, "Ovarian cancer."

There was an audible gasp in the courtroom. That was shocking and fully unexpected. But the truth can be that way.

For some, the same type of shock resonates when people meet well-qualified scientists who believe both in evolution and in the Christian faith. One finds people like Dr. Francis Collins, the American physician and geneticist who headed the human genome problem. His book *The Language of God: A Scientist Presents Evidence for Belief* was a New York Times bestseller. My friend Dr. Simon Conway-Morris is one of the world's top evolutionists at the University of Cambridge, famous forever for his work on the Burgess Shale fossils. Yet sit with him over tea, and hear him expound on his belief in the virgin birth and the God who is real.

One of my favorite authors to read is John Polkinghorne (1930–2021). Polkinghorne was a professor of mathematical physics at Queen's College, Cambridge, as well as an Anglican priest. His science propelled him to membership in the prestigious and exclusive Fellow of the Royal Society in 1974. Knighted by the Queen in 1997, Polking-horne wrote multiple books explaining how the cosmos and the Bible both expose the reality of God.

Evolution and faith are opposite choices. They can be bedfellows. The biggest reaction that many give to this statement is generally, "But doesn't the book of Genesis mean that evolution is impossible?" In short, my answer is, "No. Genesis doesn't address that question." Let's examine this.

GENESIS AND EVOLUTION

About twenty years ago, a blessing and a curse simultaneously appeared in my life. Email. In some ways, it radically altered my life for good. Before the intrusion of this never-sleeping giant, I would regularly have to telephone my office to check in and see if anything needed my attention. It meant I was on the phone almost hourly.

Once I figured out what email could do, the telephone check-ins faded into obscurity. I simply needed to check my emails. Fast forward twenty years. I get 350 daily reasons I must check my email. They pop up more regularly than fly balls at a baseball game.

Emails have brought to the surface some problems with current writing. For one, although plentiful, my fonts are limited. I have fonts that enable me to be emphatic, but I am missing fonts that indicate sarcasm. Certainly, there are folks who regularly use sarcasm, and as email became a popular channel for communicating in place of the telephone, sarcasm did not go away. It is still used. But it can be hard to detect in an email.

Email requires me to try hard to figure out the tone of one's writings. Websites operate similarly. I remember the first time someone sent me an article from *The Onion*. I was unaware that *The Onion* was a satiric website commenting on modern times and culture. While claiming to be "America's finest news source," I quickly learned it speaks only tongue-in-cheek.

Anytime I try to read something, my mind automatically tends to shift into an interpretative mode. It might be literal, it might be satirical, or it might be imaginative. When it comes to books, I generally have the benefit of the book coming from a section denoted *non-fiction* or *fiction*, but regardless, interpretation is the key.

The Bible contains an assortment of writing styles, many of which people commonly use today (narrative, historical dialogue, poetry, letters, etc.). Some of the writing styles were more common in the ancient cultures into which the Bible was written than what is in twenty-first-century America (e.g., the ancient use of chiasm). It can, at times, make it a bit difficult to understand exactly what the writers had in mind when reading some challenging passages.

This becomes important when one examines the Bible and the issue of evolution. For the Jew and the Christian, the issue centers on how to read and understand the first several chapters of the book of Genesis. These are pages that were written before "pages" came to be. They come from over three thousand years ago and likely from a language that gradually became the ancient Hebrew that molded much of the rest of the Old Testament.

For anyone, one of the key challenges is to read the creation pages from Genesis in their original cultural context, seizing on the concepts as they existed at the time of writing, to understand the message those pages were meant to convey. Then one can take the message and place it into modern language, utilizing modern concepts and under-standings of reality. Let me give an example of what I mean.

Historically, humanity observed the sun "rising" in the east and "setting" in the west. Many use those terms still today, but as a visual comment on what we see. No one really believes that the sun is ac-tually coming up from the edge of the world and coursing or moving across the sky until it recedes at the opposite edge of the world. I might speak of the sun rising, but I know that the earth is rotating, and the sun is staying relatively in one place.

So, the Bible will also speak of the rising and setting of the sun, not because the Bible is scientifically in error on cosmic geometry and motion. It is the language and mindset of the time when the Psalmist wrote, "From the rising of the sun to its setting, the name of the LORD is to be praised!" (Ps 113:3).

A primary goal in trying to assess what the Bible says about evo-lution is to determine what the Bible says about origins. One must be careful, however, for in asking what the Bible says about evolution, one is asking a twenty-first-century question of a three-thousand-year-old text. One must read the Bible in context, and I believe that as one does, one finds a great deal of liberty in deciding beliefs—whether and to what extent to believe in creation, evolution, intelligent design, or most any other meritorious scientific understanding of origins.

THE WARNINGS FROM AUGUSTINE

Augustine (AD 354–430) wrote a number of books on Genesis. He wrote two early books setting out the allegorical meaning, "not venturing to expound the deep mysteries of nature in the literal sense."[1] Later, he decided to write on the literal interpretation, but he stopped before finishing because "I collapsed under the weight of a burden I could not bear."[2] Time allowed Augustine to write many more volumes on the literal meaning of Genesis, but still, in his final works, "one will encounter more questions raised than answers found."[3]

Consider, for example, Augustine's writing on what Genesis means by "God called the light Day and the darkness Night." Augustine could not figure out how there would be light/day followed by darkness/night. Although he did not understand that the world was a globe, he did understand that the sun never truly went "out," but instead shone over other places on earth. Without scientific certainty, yet challenging the apparent worldview of Genesis 1, Augustine wrote,

> But if I make such a statement, I fear I shall be laughed at both by those who have scientific knowledge of these matters and by those who can easily recognize the facts of the case. At the time when night is with us, the sun is illuminating with its presence those parts of the world through which it returns from the place of its setting to that of its rising. Hence it is that for the whole twenty-four hours of the sun's circuit there is always day in one place and night in another.[4]

Many find Genesis 1 and 2 perplexing chapters to understand literally. Some struggle to see how there was "day" and "night" or "evening" and "morning" (day one) before God made the "greater light to rule the day" and "the lesser light to rule the night" (day four). For that matter, how does the earth sprout vegetation, fruit trees, and other plants the day before (day three) he apparently makes the sun? Over the centuries, these issues have brought forth a number of suggested answers that satisfy some, but not all.[5]

Those questions were hard on Augustine, and science has not made them easier. Now that people understand that night and day stem from the earth revolving around the sun, one might similarly wonder how the earth was rotating day and night without a sun to revolve around.

I want to consider what Genesis says, but even more, what it does not say. For I have a range of ways in which to understand Genesis and still hold to an authoritative view of Scripture as inerrantly conveying what God wishes to convey in the way God wishes to convey it. There is comfort and warning in Augustine's words,

> In matters that are obscure and far beyond our vision, even in such as we may find treated in Holy Scripture, different interpretations are sometimes possible without prejudice to the faith we have received. In such a case, we should not rush in headlong and so firmly take our stand on one side that, if further progress in the search for truth justly undermines this position, we too fall with it. That would be to battle not for the teaching of Holy Scripture but for our own, wishing its teaching to conform to ours, whereas we ought to wish ours to conform to that of Sacred Scripture.[6]

So with that admonition, I begin by trying to understand the Genesis account, and then I consider the teachings of science.

WHAT DOES GENESIS SAY ABOUT GOD AND EVOLUTION?

The creation material in Genesis 1:1–2:3 is worthy of a massive, multi-hundred-page tome—more than a few pages in this chapter. Exhaustive material cannot be presented in this limited format, so my goal is directed differently. The point of this section is to explain why the concepts of science, evolution, and the like do not drive me away from a belief in God or the Bible. For the atheist or agnostic to place me in a box of thinking I must embrace either God or science is not fair. I can and do fully embrace both, and I believe the Bible does as well.

With that goal in mind, and with the limitations of space, here I consider certain aspects of the Genesis passage relevant to the discussion at hand and leave aside some of the more detailed debates.

For example, there is a debate among scholars as to whether the first line in Genesis should be translated, "In the beginning, God created the heavens and the earth" (ESV) or something like, "When God began to create heaven and earth."[7] Although there are some implications for the creation/evolution dialogue in which translations are chosen, it is not so significant that I dwell on it here. I merely note that there are plenty of places to study it.[8] My examination is met by setting out enough of the creation passage to give it context and, in the process, address several of the more cited areas of dispute.

At first glance, it might seem as if there are two different creation stories. In fact, many biblical scholars assert that there are. Genesis 1–2:3 speak of the seven days of God's creation and rest. God made light and separated it from darkness on day one. On day two, God made an expanse called "heaven" and separated the waters above from the waters below. The third day, God took the waters below the expanse (below heaven) and gathered them into one place so that dry land appeared. God called the land "earth" and the waters "seas." God then had the earth bring forth vegetation, plants yielding seed, and fruit trees.

On day four, God set lights in the heavens to separate day and night, and to establish seasons. God specifically made the two great lights, the sun to rule the day, and the moon to rule the night, as well as the stars, setting them in the expanse called heaven. On day five, God created great sea creatures and every living creature that moves in the water. God also made the birds that inhabit the sky. God blessed the creatures and said for them to be fruitful and multiply.

Day six is when God created the living creatures of the earth. God then made people after his own likeness and in his image. God created humanity as male and female. As with the fish and birds, God issued the command to be fruitful and multiply. Day seven is a day without creation; it is the day God rested. God blessed the seventh day and made it holy.

This is the story through Genesis 2:3. Then in Genesis 2:4, it seems to some that a second creation story is given. No longer is "God" the acting subject, but now it is the "Lord God" (adding "Yahweh"—Lord— to the Hebrew for "God"). Chapter two speaks of the Lord God making man at a time "when no bush of the field was yet in the land and no small plant of the field had yet sprung up—for the Lord God had not caused it to rain on the land, and there was no man to work the ground, and a mist was going up from the land and was watering the whole face of the ground" (Gen 2:5-6).

While God does not provide rain until the flood of Noah, he does make man before vegetation. The Lord God creates man from the dust of the ground, breathes the breath of life into his nostrils, and *then* plants a garden in Eden, placing man there. "Adam" (the Hebrew word for "man") is given the charge of working the garden. In chapter one, God made plants on day three, and man on day six. Chapter two seems to reverse the order with man coming *before* plants. This adds to the consideration that perhaps the stories reflect two different traditions. If not two different stories, then perhaps there is a writing style that is calling into emphasis different points and helping inform how the stories should be read.

Closer examination of the creation passages brings out several important things. First, one should note that Genesis 1–2:3 is written in a different form or style from the rest of Genesis. The "seven days" passages are written in what one scholar has termed "exalted prose narrative."[9]

The passages take a repetitive form that is structured quite beautifully. Day after day begins with, "And God said . . ." (Gen 1:3, 6, 9, 11, 14, 20, 24, 26). That is repeatedly followed by a statement, "Let there be . . ." (Gen 1:3, 6, 14) or simply "Let the . . ." (Gen 1:9, 11, 20, 24). Whatever God had declared to happen then occurs, and God notes that it is "good" (Gen 1:4, 10, 12, 18, 21, 25), and then at the end of his creating, "very good" (Gen 1:31). After each day's creating work, "evening" comes, followed by "morning" (Gen 1:5, 8, 13, 19, 23, 31). Finally, one sees that something is missing from this regimental repetition. On the seventh day, there is no note of "evening and morning following the activity of the day" (God's rest).

There is another interesting aspect to the creation days. They fall into two easily discernable categories, those of "forming" and "filling." On days one, two, and three, God forms. Then on days four, five, and six, he fills those forms. See the relationship in figure 11.1.

FORMING	FILLING
Day 1: light (day) and darkness (night) **Day 2:** heavens and waters **Day 3:** earth/vegetation	**Day 4:** the sun (filling day) the moon/stars (filling night) **Day 5:** birds (filling heaven) fish (filling waters) **Day 6:** animals and man (filling earth and eating vegetation)

Figure 11.1. During the days of creation, God either forms something or fills something

This takes on greater significance when one sees the verses before the days of creation where it reads, "In the beginning, God created the heavens and the earth. The earth was *without form* and *void*" (Gen 1:1-2, emphasis added). The heavens and earth are made, but they are formless and void. Then for three days God forms the heavens and earth, followed by three days where he fills the voids in those forms.

Again, as with the absence of evening and morning, day seven is different. It is neither a forming nor a filling. It is a holy day of rest. Reading these days in this structure shows God's carefully planned provisions for his people. He first builds good habitats and then fills them.

In Genesis 2:4, is the first of eleven verses in Genesis to bear the Hebrew refrain, *toledot*. This Hebrew word often carries the translation, "These are the generations of . . ." Over and over, it seems to indicate a focus on material that follows as a narrowing of attention on a matter set out earlier. One might consider it as a modern chapter heading.[10] This is one of many factors that lead scholars to see the creation focus in Genesis 2 as a microscope that intensifies the focus on the creation of man and woman, rather than simply a second or independent tradition of creation.

Once one reaches this part of the creation text, the writing shifts from the highly exalted, almost poetic structure of Genesis 1:1–2:3, and becomes ordinary Hebrew prose.

INTERPRETATIONS

How should one fairly understand these passages in Genesis? That makes the critical difference in whether they are at odds with science. Are they literal? If so, *how* literal? If they are not literal, what are they?

"Literal." I put literal in quotes because it takes different forms in the minds of different people. Some believe that God literally made the world in six successive twenty-four-hour days, followed by a twenty-four-hour day of rest.[11] Typically, this view also takes the genealogies and associated dating in Genesis 5 as literal as well, resulting in a view that the earth is somewhere around six thousand years old. Such a view seems immediately at odds with the geologic and archaeologic records, with cities over ten thousand years old and dinosaurs reaching far back before that.

Others take this section as literal, holding to six twenty-four-hour days, but not necessarily considering the days successive. In this view, great time periods might have existed between the various days of creation. This is also called the "intermittent day view."

Still, another view that holds to a literal interpretation has been termed the "gap theory." This view focuses on the first two verses of Genesis: "In the beginning, God created the heavens and the earth. The earth was without form and void, and darkness was over the face of the deep. And the Spirit of God was hovering over the face of the waters."

These verses are seen not as simply a prelude or introduction to the verses of chapter one. Instead, they are interpreted as an independent aspect of creation that took place a considerable time before the six days of creation. God created the heavens and the earth, all sorts of history occurred, and then came a destruction that left a formless void of darkness. Into this came God with the creation detailed in the following verses.

A literal view, more so than other views, can be seen to set the biblical story at odds with what science teaches in origins. An oft-cited example is, how can one have vegetation (day three) before the sun (day four)? Of course, there is always the recourse to the God who can do it anyway he chooses. However, I should note that an interesting aspect of the literal interpretation is often overlooked. Namely, the passages say that the earth was told to bring forth vegetation and plants, animals, birds, and fish, but it does not tell "*how* the earth 'brought forth vegetation' or how the animals appeared in their respective environments."[12]

This has brought some to believe that the six creation days are listed in an artistic order rather than the order of creation. The numbers assigned are not seen as sequential but rather as identifying tags. An example of this is given in comparing Matthew's account of the temptation of Jesus with Luke's. Matthew has Jesus tempted first with hunger, then at the pinnacle of the temple, then with the kingdoms of the world (Mt 4:1-10). In Luke, the order of the last two temptations is flipped. Luke has the hunger, the kingdoms, and *then* the pinnacle of the temple (Lk 4:1-13). This, it is argued, is an example of how the Bible can record history accurately but change the ordering of events to make a point.

A change in order in Genesis is frequently seen as setting up the "form/filling" structure. In that regard, Collins writes, "We may simply conclude from this high level of patterning that the order of events and even lengths of time are not part of the author's focus. . . . In this understanding, the six workdays are a literary device to display the creation week as a careful and artful effort."[13]

Collins later adds that he sees "the highly patterned form of this pericope [the form/filling texts] as evidence that the reader is invited to sit lightly on sequence and time lengths." I cite Collins repeatedly, not because he is alone on an island with his views. Rather, he is mainstream even among the most zealous for an "inerrancy" view of the Bible. One of evangelicalism's leading and most outspoken inerrantists, J. I. Packer, recommends Collins's commentary as a "model of good reading of the text."[14]

Day/age. A second view, which is fairly called "literal" as well, is that which considers the Hebrew word for "day" in the first chapter to mean an "era," or an "age" as opposed to a twenty-four-hour day. This view stems from the fact that the Hebrew word for "day" (*yom*) can mean a twenty-four-hour day, an era or age, or even more limited, it can mean the time of daylight.[15] The English word is used similarly today. Scripture does teach, of course, that God is outside of time. As a result, earth's "days" are certainly not the same to him (Ps 90:4; 2 Pet 3:8).

To make such a determination in Scripture, the scholar or student needs to look at the context. In the framework of Genesis, there are two dominant aspects to the text that are cited favorably by those who ascribe to this view. First is the description given for the seventh "day." That is the only day where the day does not end. The other six days have the conclusion that would have followed the workday of any Jew, evening and morning.[16] But on the seventh day, Scripture says that God blessed it, and made it holy because he rested on that day. It was not followed by evening and morning.

Many understand this to mean that people still live in the seventh day, the day (or age) of God's rest. In this sense, Hebrews 4:3-11 is used to show the idea that believers "enter God's rest" as opposed to those who do not get that blessing: "For we who have believed enter that rest, as he has said. . . . For he has somewhere spoken of the seventh day in this way: "And God rested on the seventh day from all his works." . . . So then, there remains a Sabbath rest for the people of God, for whoever has entered God's rest has also rested from his works as God did from his."

This view that the seventh day was not simply twenty-four hours but an age/era carries over to the other days as well.

A second indication that is used to justify the age/era interpretation is found in Genesis 2:4: "These are the generations of the heavens and the earth when they were created, in the *day* that the LORD God made the earth and the heavens." This passage then goes on to speak of the creation of man, the creation of plants (or the planting of the Garden of Eden), naming all the animals, searching for a mate, the deep sleep of man, and the creation of woman. Those events, it is argued, did not all occur within twenty-four hours, and this indicates that *day* is meaning something more.

Allegorical. Another way that the creation passages have found interpretation by those who adhere to a high view of Scripture is as allegory. This was especially prominent in the early church in Alexandria, Egypt.[17] In that time and place in church history, those who read the story as simple literal history were deemed to be placing a lower view on Scripture's inspiration, for common people could write history. God would have written something much deeper, so it was reasoned.

The main advantage of taking the passages allegorically is that there is then no problem with any consistency or scientific challenge. Once the road of allegory is chosen, some might say that anything goes. Of course, that is also the main disadvantage to taking it allegorically— anything goes! Can there be certainty of anything, unless somewhere Scripture gives the allegorical interpretation? This view has not kept the prominence it once enjoyed in the early church, but it is not without adherents today.[18]

Even some who take a literal understanding at times see allegorical understandings of the texts. Much like Augustine, they question how the passages make sense unless the "light" created includes an idea of the spiritual insight God creates in an individual.

A related idea is to see the account, at least of Genesis 1:1–2:3 as a poetic expression of God's theological message rather than a recitation of science or history. Hence the pattern of the days as form and filling, the parallel structure of the writing, is seen as an indicator of an artistic painting rather than a historical recording. Much like the Psalms that sometimes use poetry and picture to paint images, the passage in Genesis 1:1–2:3 is read for its message over its history. This view melds quickly into the next view I consider.

Historical context. The "historical context" approach to Scripture seems most intellectually honest to me. It means to draw a passage's meaning first in light of how it would have been understood in its own day. One must understand the text first as written in the language and culture of the initial recipients.

Scripture indicates that the Israelites were cognizant of the culture around them. For example, they often strayed into the idol worship of their neighbors, constantly fighting to return to the worship of God (see 2 Kings 11:18-28). Similarly, they sought a king because "all the nations" had one (1 Sam 8:5). One should expect that the Jews would be aware of the origins and creation stories of their neighbors.

Israel had spent four hundred years in Egypt and doubtlessly absorbed some of that culture and perspective. In addition to Egyptian myths, other contemporary stories and ideas placed before ancient Israel are still known today thanks, in part, to the Assyrian King Ashurbanipal.

In the seventh century BC, King Ashurbanipal (668–627 BC) ruled in his hot, dry capital city of Nineveh (modern-day northern Iraq). The king had a tremendous library with thousands of clay tablets, the "books" of his day. These tablets covered almost every subject, from the mundane to the fanciful (legal tablets, transactional tablets, etc.). In time, the king died, his empire crumbled, and dirt conquered his library, burying the building and its contents. Then, in the mid- to late 1800s, archaeologists discovered these tablets, and scholarship of the Old Testament has never been the same. These books provide insight into several areas, including multiple creation myths of Israel's neighbors.

In the creation stories of the *Atrahasis* and the *Enuma Elish*, one reads how the gods were created. The gods' first efforts are to fight chaos and bring order to the world. As the gods continue to multiply, they do all sorts of human things, though on a grander, more god-like scale. There are working gods who dig the Tigris and Euphrates rivers, piling up the dirt into mountains. There are warring gods, who fight against each other, at one point hacking a dead goddess into two and hurling half of her body into the sky to form the dome of heaven.

In these stories of Israel's neighbors, the gods each have possession over the aspects of creation they either made or came to own. So the god who owns the storms has jurisdiction and control over the weather. The god of the sea is the sea. The god who has possession of a certain area of the earth can be both in that earth and presiding over that part of earth. Typically, in these stories, gods make people to relieve the burdens from the gods. The toil involved in the gods' hard work on earth starts to wear on them.

Radically, into a culture and community of this sort comes a creation story that is as opposite as possible. There is one God, not many. God is not made; he is the maker. God does not war against chaos to bring order; God creates the world in an orderly fashion, forming and filling in ways that are "very good." God does not simply make one aspect of creation to inhabit and rule over. God makes all of creation. He makes everything. God is not relegated to a certain piece of real estate; he presides over all there is. Creation is not a part of God, nor an aspect of his body. Creation is independent of God, something he spoke into being.

God did not grow weary of creating. He was not challenged in digging creeks and rivers or in building mountains. God made all with simple words. He rested not out of fatigue, but because his work was finished, and it was "very good"!

People were made not to relieve God of burdens; people were made in God's image to enjoy his fellowship and company. In the words of John Collins, "God made the material world as a place for mankind to live: to love, to work, to enjoy, and to worship God. The exalted tone of the passage allows the reader to ponder this with a sense of awe, adoring the goodness, power, and creativity of the One who did all this."[19]

The historical context view sees the Genesis account as setting out the truth of God and his creation, not in the sense of science and history, but in the sense of story that teaches a competing truth to the stories surrounding the Israelites.

Peter Enns has another way of expressing the historical context perspective. Enns expounded on a view set forth by Patterson Smyth in the late 1800s that Enns has termed the "incarnational analogy." Enns writes that just "as Christ is both God and human, so is the Bible."[20] Enns then points out that Christ came into a culture using the language of the people, the manners of the people, the customs of the people, and was "made like his brothers in every way" (Heb 2:17). So too, Enns sees the Bible: "Because Christianity is a historical religion, God's word reflects the various historical moments in which Scripture was written. God acted and spoke in history."[21]

He sees the fact that the Bible was written in common tongue, the ordinary human language of the day, as substantiating his position. So Enns sees the Genesis texts as likely intended to contrast stories like the *Enuma Elish*. Enns does not believe the focus should be "history vs. myth" but rather "message vs. message."[22]

This section is not necessarily exclusive from other interpretive views. Many holding other views recognize that the proper starting place for understanding the passage is the message's meaning to its first audience. That said, Enns argues against a literal/scientific view believing it would be a misunderstanding to make Genesis a scientific view. In his mind, "It is wholly incomprehensible to think that thousands of years ago God would have felt constrained to speak in a way that would be meaningful only to Westerners several thousand years later. To do so borders on modern, western arrogance."[23] Of course, contrary to Enns's belief, most who hold to a literal/scientific view would not agree that the message speaks only to those of the scientific era.

Wheaton College professor John Walton sets out the various worldviews, the cultural mores, and the competing belief systems of the ancient Near East to give original sense to the Genesis stories. He notes that God is communicating in the stories, but,

> Effective communication requires a body of agreed-upon words, terms, and ideas. . . . For the speaker [God] this often requires accommodation to the audience. One uses words (representing ideas) that the audience will understand, thus, by definition, accommodating to the target audience. . . . As interpreters, then, we must adapt to the language/culture matrix of the ancient world as we study the Old Testament.[24]

Put in the context of creation, Walton asserts that comparative studies (comparing Genesis to other stories like the *Enuma Elish* or *Atrahasis*) are important for three reasons. First, they give more data to help understand the text. Second, they also help defend the authenticity of the text as it fits into its age in Scripture. Third, they provide insight into the exegesis of the passage.

Walton notes that comparing the creation stories to the Babylonian and Assyrian myths gives a number of distinctions. Walton argues that the Jews had a similar view of the cosmos to those of other contemporary cultures. He explains a three-tiered cosmos with water locked in the heavens above the hard inverted shell that is the sky. Clouds cover the "windows" that open up in the sky allowing some of the heavenly waters to fall upon "earth." Mountains hold up the sky. The sky has the track for the sun, moon, and stars. Earth itself is a disc that sits on pillars above other waters. Underneath the waters and the earth is the underworld. Walton asserts that this worldview is in the Genesis creation account as God spoke to the early Jews in their language and mindsets.

These many different approaches to Genesis immediately remove the issue of "faith versus evolution." The fact that one does or does not believe in evolution does not impinge on the biblical understanding of God. It might influence how one understands the passages, but it is not at odds with the passages.

CLOSING
ARGUMENT

IF YOU HAVE MADE IT THIS FAR in this book, you have seen the approach I would use in the courtroom to examine unbelief—whether atheism or agnosticism. Either that or you chose to cut to the chase and head straight for the summation chapter. Either way, you likely have an interest in ultimate questions.

Since at least high school, I have tried to figure out the world. I want to know why things are the way they are and how they came to be. Part of that is knowing why I am the way I am. Why I think as I do, why I have my shortcomings, most of which I feel useless to conquer, why I have a longing for love, why I have a sense of right and wrong, why injustice grates at me, why I am attracted by that which I deem noble: these are the questions I want answered.

In trying to answer those questions, I realized early that a proper and compelling view of reality would answer my questions in a coherent and consistent way. I do not expect to come up with an entirely new worldview. For thousands of years many of humanity's brightest minds have asked similar questions and formed worldviews. In a sense, my job is akin to going to a supermarket of ideas. I can shop through many different opinions to decide which makes the most sense to me.

That shopping trip through ideas is what took me to examine atheism and agnosticism. I wanted to sift through the bin of answers to life's questions and see whether those systems of skepticism and unbelief satisfy with answers.

The answers of atheism and agnosticism don't satisfy me, however. They fall woefully short. Those answers are like Prince Charming trying to wedge Cinderella's slipper onto the feet of her stepsisters. The contortions involved trying to fit those ideas onto the real world where I live are beyond one's mental gymnastics skills. The ideas simply don't match up with reality.

I touched on these issues in *Christianity on Trial*. In response, I got an unsolicited comment from a gentleman in Canada. Through email, he challenged my view that atheism strips one of objective ethics and meaning. A chemist by training, he was adamant that science could provide explanations for everything. He saw faith as requiring a repulsion of all the science he held so dear. As I walked through my views of Scripture, he at first scoffed, then rebuffed, then finally came to realize that I was not running from Scripture but fairly expounding and explaining it.

Through months of email correspondence, I learned this man was a moral and caring father and husband. But my persistent challenge to him was to explain *why* he thought is morally imperative to be that way. Without a God, I asserted, his life was an illusion of meaning. We went back and forth, challenging the ideas and logic of each other. The most delightful email I got was his telling me about coming to faith. His joy exploded off the screen as I read of his new reality. God's meaning makes a real difference.

I know that the answers to life must be consistent with life. I can't argue the moon is made of cheese when I know better. I can't assert that I am well when I have a fever of 102, a runny nose, a sore throat, headache, lost sense of smell and taste, and a positive test for the presence of Covid-19. I may tell myself and others I am well, but I'm not. I am sick, and it would be wrong of me to be around others and infect them. In the same sense, I am insistent that my view of the world be consistent with the reality I live and see in others. My answers to life's questions must be firmly planted in the reality of life.

So I weigh the options as I weigh the evidence. I examine the answers provided by those who put their faith in unbelief. I see what the atheist believes. I consider the belief system defaulted to by agnostics. I assess the criticisms of theism, seeing if belief in God provides answers missing by skepticism. When I do, I find that the Judeo-Christian faith fits life snugly. The faith explains not only my life but also the lives of atheists and agnostics. Cinderella's shoe fits Cinderella's foot.

How do I get there? As in any trial, it is simple. I follow the evidence. I weigh the evidence that supports each worldview and I embrace the one that makes the most sense. When I do that, I find insurmountable obstacles to "unbelief" being factual.

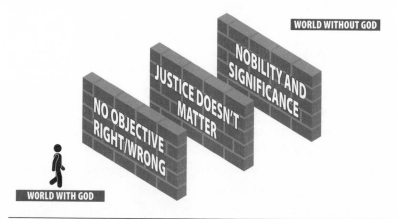

Figure 12.1. For me to live in a world where there is no God, I would need to overcome my inherent realization that there is a measure of objective right and wrong, that justice and fairness are virtues, and that the nobility and significance of humanity is real

Chief among the obstacles is the sense of justice, fairness, and morality. In the worldview options, I must explain why I care so intrinsically about morality and fairness.

The worldviews see me as one of two things: either (1) I am a sack of chemicals, that time and chance have formed from space dust relegated to this outback corner of an immense galaxy in a vast universe; or (2) I am the result of a divine decision to form a species that reflects a measure of the Divine.

If I am the former, as a bag of chemicals, I have no basis for believing that ultimate morality is anything other than a charade. Under this system, anything goes. My life is abjectly arbitrary, a chance occurrence that is both meaningless and dismal. Of course, some atheists who might read this would protest. They would say, "No! Not so! One can be an atheist and care about justice and right versus wrong." I would expect an atheist to say that because I do not believe an atheist is truly simply a sack of chemicals and stardust. Because we are human beings imprinted with God's morality, ethics, meaning, and love, all of these will mean something, even to the atheists. They are hardwired in a way that embeds the universe's planner, whether they believe it or not.

This book is published in a post-Covid-19 world. While that tragic disease coursed through humans around the globe, many people were infected. I know of several who were infected but refused to believe it. They thought the whole disease was a hoax. They were carriers, infecting others perhaps, but never admitting it to be true. It reminded me of the atheist living in a world that only makes sense with a Christian worldview. The atheist believes their worldview is right, much like some believed they lived virus free. Yet reality proves otherwise.

The very fact that most atheists and agnostics would refute the idea that their belief system leads to nothingness in the world of morality tells you that they are hardwired under a different worldview. They may think they live in a world with no God, but they live in a world with God! This means that their lives are in tension with their professed beliefs. While they would like to embrace their atheism, their lifestyle dictates another reality.

Consider this analogy from the world of physics. If you take two magnets, each magnet will have a "positive pole" and a "negative pole."

The positive pole of one magnet will attract the negative pole of the second magnet. Put those magnets together with that alignment of poles, and the magnets will cling tightly. But while the opposite poles attract, the same poles will repel each other. If you try to push the positive pole of one magnet to the positive pole of the second magnet, the magnets will force themselves apart. Try as you might, the two magnets cannot align and cling on the same poles.

So it is with the worldview you and I have. I can choose mentally to believe the world is one where there is a God or one where there is no God.

COMPETING VIEWS OF REALITY AND THE WORLD

Figure 12.2. I can make a mental choice to decide which worldview is true, or "in which reality I live." However, my real life, as opposed to my mental thoughts, live in a world explained only by the worldview of a biblical God. I can no more live my life in the worldview of no God than a magnet can attract on the same poles. Every time I try to live in the worldview of no god, the truth will force my life in perceptible ways into the true worldview. I can't escape living with a recognition that some things are wrong, unfair, unjust, etc. I can't escape living with the significance of human life beyond being cosmic stardust.

I have choices. You have choices. Think through a system of belief based on reality, and then live consistently with it. If you do, the solution won't be cosmic sacks of chemicals. Humanity is special. One will rightly get upset over the needless slaughter of the innocents. The death of Aunt Bessie is never justification for feeding her corpse to pigs. I can't turn my head when someone is abusing a child. People are not the same as sharks in the ocean, feeding indiscriminately on whatever swims in their path. The Christian worldview of people hardwired by God to be moral, to care about justice, to appreciate the noble, to seek alleviation of misery, to be curious and learn, to use the tools of nature and science to make the world a better place—these things make sense to me.

I similarly better understand why I am inadequate. I do not measure up to the God who fashioned me. I have issues of self-control. I tend to put myself in the middle of the universe. I seek after things I shouldn't. I fail to do the right thing, even when I want to. The Christian view of humanity's fall into the sticky trap of sin is a reality of my daily existence.

The Christian promise of a forgiving and merciful, yet fully just God makes sense to me. It has given me the peace of heart that allows me to exist and thrive in this life. I have purpose, insight, and satisfaction, even in the midst of inadequacy. My relationship with the God who is there makes my life make sense and imbues me with hope and confidence for tomorrow. I challenge anyone wondering about this to consider my companion book, *Christianity on Trial*. In it, I consider these fundamentals of the Christian answers to life's questions more fully.

But in summation to my examination of atheism and agnosticism, I find them inadequate explanations of reality. They don't explain what I see, and they would not survive cross-examination in the courtroom of truth.

ACKNOWLEDGMENTS

A BOOK LIKE THIS DOESN'T COME TOGETHER EASILY, and I have many to thank for help along the way. My wife, Becky, and our children, Will, Gracie, Rachel, Rebecca, and Sarah, have all contributed through conversations with ideas, challenges, and inspiration. My mom ("Mimi") taught me some of the most formative ideas in this book from an earliest age. My sisters, Kathryn and Hollie, have supported and informed this work as only sisters who walk closely with the Lord are able.

Beyond family, the folks at the Biblical Literacy class at Champion Forest Baptist Church who listened as I taught this material, with many offering insights and provoking through thoughtful questioning, helped mold this book. Especially notable among them I want to thank Pastor David Fleming, Dr. Janet Siefert, Pastor Brent Johnson, and Dale Hearn, as each of them contributed much.

I also thank and acknowledge the people at the Lanier Theological Library, notably Charles Mickey, who offered insights into early lessons that became this book, and Dr. David Capes, who carefully scrutinized each page, fixing verb tenses as well as theology!

Dr. Michael Lloyd, Principal at Wycliffe Hall Oxford, was especially helpful on the problem of evil chapter, and I thank him also.

My nephew, Dr. Jack Hunt, made sure I got my nomenclature and science right on "seeing things," and was quick to pull from PubMed when I needed. Thank you, nephew!

Thank you to the amazing people at InterVarsity Press, including senior editor Al Hsu, who saw fit to not only publish this book but to expand it beyond my original intentions, thereby producing this single volume dedicated to examining unbelief.

To God be the glory.

NOTES

1. A LEGAL PRIMER

[1]*Daubert v. Merrell Dow Pharmaceuticals*, 509 U.S. 579 (1993).

2. OPENING STATEMENT

[1]G. A. Miller, "Informavores," in *The Study of Information: Interdisciplinary Messages*, ed. Machlup and Mansfield (Wiley 1983), 111-13.

[2]A common translation of the German "*Die Religion . . . ist das Opium des Volks*," in Karl Marx, introduction to *Zur Kritik der Hegel'schen Rechts-Philosophie* (1843).

[3]As an aside, the trial lawyer in me always wondered why the prosecution asked OJ to try on the glove while he was already wearing another "protective" glove, hence making it unlikely any fitting glove would still fit.

[4]*Religions on Trial* (Downers Grove, IL: InterVarsity Press, 2022).

[5]Mark Lanier, *Christianity on Trial* (Downers Grove, IL: InterVarsity Press, 2014).

[6]Biblically, God is not a gendered being. The Bible references him most often using masculine terms like *father* but not to the exclusion of also using maternal expressions (e.g., Is 49:14-16). For convention's sake, I use the more common masculinized pronouns for God.

[7]John Calvin wrote of the necessity of using human terms to speak of the divine, and is generally associated with the idea of "language of accommodation." See, e.g., *Institutes of the Christian Religion* 1.13.1. Kibbe defines Calvin's idea as "God's adjusting himself to human limitations." Michael Kibbe, "'Present and Accommodated For': Calvin's God on Mount Sinai," *Journal of Theological Interpretation* 7, no. 1 (2013): 115.

3. ATHEISM AND THE BURDEN OF PROOF

[1]"What Is Atheism?," www.atheists.org/activism/resources/about-atheism/, accessed April 1, 2021, emphasis original.

[2]John Gray, *Seven Types of Atheism* (New York: Picador, 2018), 2.

[3]*Knowledge* and *belief* have specific meanings that are often confused. By strictest definition, *knowledge* references something I *know* to be true, while *belief* references something I think is likely true. One might say, "I *know* two plus two is four." Yet one would rightly say, "I believe there is a God." Those strict definitions can be confusing when working with the meaning of words like *agnostic* which linguistically references a "knowledge" in the etymology of the word, even though we might be more proper to say an agnostic doesn't "believe" there is a God. "γνῶσις," Henry G. Liddell, Robert Scott, Henry S. Jones, and Roderick McKenzie, *A Greek-English Lexicon* (Oxford: Clarendon Press, 1940).

[4]These terms are important to understanding modern discussions on this subject. Some bright people confuse these terms, making illogical arguments in the process.

[5]*Ingham v. Johnson & Johnson*, 608 S.W.3d 663 (Mo. Ct. App. 2020), *reh'g and/or transfer denied* (July 28, 2020), *transfer denied* (Nov. 3, 2020), *cert. denied*, 20-1223, 2021 WL 2194948 (U.S. June 1, 2021).

[6]Richard Dawkins, *The Selfish Gene* (Oxford: Oxford University Press, 2006), 198.

[7]Gray, *Seven Types of Atheism*, 9, 14.

[8]See, e.g., the writings of John H. Walton, including *The Lost World of Genesis One: Ancient Cosmology and the Origins Debate* (Downers Grove, IL: InterVarsity Press, 2009).

[9]Richard Dawkins, *The God Delusion* (New York: Bantam, 2008), 322.

[10]Dawkins, *God Delusion*, 334.

[11]C. S. Lewis proposes another glaring problem in arguments like this set forward by Dawkins. In chapter three of Lewis's masterful work *Mere Christianity*, Lewis explains that God exists outside of time. If time is a string that stretches from 8 gazillion BC until 2050 (set any times you choose), the God outside of time sees the entire string at once. For God, there would be no difference in 1960, the year I was born, and 2022, the year of this book's first publishing. Furthermore, because God exists outside of time, at any precise moment of history, God has an eternity before the next nanosecond occurs. All to say, Dawkins and other who set forward this argument as proof there is no God have failed to achieve anything more than proving there is no God of the limitations and types ascribed by Dawkins.

[12]*Oxford English Dictionary*, 2nd. ed. (Oxford: Oxford University Press, 1991), 4:1012, s.v. "dragon."

[13]Dawkins, *God Delusion*, chap. 2.

[14]Bertrand Russell, *The Collected Papers of Bertrand Russell* (London: Routledge 1997), 11:547-48. Note the subtle way Russell equates belief in God as an absurdity, while atheism is sensible. Then Russell suggests that the absurd who believe in God might go so far in their zeal as to suggest that the sensible and rational unbeliever requires a psychiatrist, or in another age, might meet with the atrocities of the Inquisition. Russell is subtle in his rhetorical sleight of hand, placing modern believers in camp with the Inquisition.

4. ATHEIST ARGUMENTS

[1]Sam Harris, *The End of Faith: Religion, Terror, and the Future of Reason* (New York: W. W. Norton, 2004), 16-18.

[2]Harris, *End of Faith*, 16.

[3]Harris, *End of Faith*, 17.

[4]Harris, *End of Faith*, 18.

[5]See Larry R. Morrison, "The Religious Defense of American Slavery Before 1830," *The Journal of Religious Thought* 37 (1980–1981).

[6]C. MacFarlane and T. Thompson, *The Comprehensive History of England, from the Earliest Period to the Suppression of the Sepoy Revolt* (London, 1876), 752.

[7]Charles Spurgeon, "The Secret Spot," *The Christian Cabinet*, December 14, 1859.

[8]John Wesley, "Thoughts Upon Slavery," in *The Works of John Wesley* (London, 1774), 11:76.

[9]See, e.g., the writings at the Richard Dawkins Foundation for Reason & Science with an article by Michael Sherlock, "The Atheist Atrocities Fallacy," October 23, 2014, www.richarddawkins.net/2014/10/the-atheist-atrocities-fallacy-hitler -stalin-pol-pot/. Sherlock gets this from a speech Hitler gave in public. Note to reader: don't believe everything a politician says to sway public opinion!

[10]Adolf Hitler, *Hitler's Table Talk, 1941–1944: His Private Conversations*, trans. Norman Cameron and R.H. Stevens (New York: Enigma, 2008), 80.

[11]Hitler, *Hitler's Table Talk, 1941–1944*, 152.

[12]Jonathan Brent, *Inside the Stalin Archives: Discovering the New Russia* (New York: Atlas, 2008), 3.

[13]Yemelyan Yaroslavsky, *Landmarks in the Life of Stalin* (London: Lawrence and Wishart, 1942).

[14]Martin Luther, *Works of Martin Luther: With Introductions and Notes* (Philadelphia: A. J. Holman, 1915), 2:173.

[15]This argument is also set out by the four horsemen, especially in debates. The reason is not so much to argue that there is no God, but to argue that Christianity and biblical concepts of God are dangerous, inconsistent, or immoral. That is a

different thrust of the argument and worthy of its own book. It has no bearing on whether there is a God. It bears on what kind of God he or she might be. In this regard I refer the interested reader to my book *Christianity on Trial* (Downers Grove, IL: InterVarsity Press, 2014).

[16]K. Y. Cha and D. P. Wirth, "Does Prayer Influence the Success of In Vitro Fertilization-Embryo Transfer? Report of a Masked, Randomized Trial," *Journal of Reproductive Medicine* 46, no. 9 (2001): 781-87.

[17]J. A. Astin et al., "The Efficacy of 'Distant Healing': A Systematic Review of Randomized Trials," *Annals of Internal Medicine* 132, no. 11 (2000): 903-10.

[18]This is much the same answer I give when Dawkins, Hitchens, Harris, and others cite arguments of religious people and then attack them. I quickly say, "Don't ascribe those to me! Those are arguments of 'Christians' who are not thinking things through carefully enough!"

5. AGNOSTICISM, EVIDENCE, AND THE BIG QUESTIONS

[1]Sir Austin Bradford Hill (1897–1991) was a British epidemiologist and statistician. He pioneered the science behind moving a relationship from "association" to "causation." His model employed nine criteria termed variously: (1) strength or effect size; (2) consistency or reproducibility; (3) site specificity; (4) temporality or time of occurrence; (5) biological gradient or dose response relationship; (6) plausibility; (7) coherence; (8) experiment; and (9) analogy. Not all criteria are necessary, but employing these, Hill is credited in proving that tobacco usage wasn't merely associated with lung cancer, but it caused lung cancer. See generally Austin Bradford Hill, "The Environment and Disease: Association or Causation?," *Proceedings of the Royal Society of Medicine* 58, no. 5 (1965): 295-300.

6. MORALITY, BEAUTY, AND JUSTICE

[1]Nick Bostrom, "Are You Living in a Computer Simulation?," *Philosophical Quarterly* 53, no. 111 (2003), 243.

[2]Joshua Rothman, "What Are the Odds We Are Living in a Computer Simulation?," *The New Yorker*, June 9, 2016.

[3]René Descartes published his now-famous *Discourse on Method* in 1637 asserting "*Cogito ergo sum*" ("I think, therefore, I am"). He reasoned that even if a demon tricked him into thinking he existed, then he must exist in order to be tricked!

[4]Thomas Nagel, *The View from Nowhere* (Oxford: Oxford University Press, 1986), 138.

[5]Plato wrote the dialogue between Socrates and Euthyphro, placing it weeks before Socrates' trial and execution in 399 BC. The classic English translation with the Greek text provided as well is found in the Loeb Classical Library

volume 36, edited and translated by Christopher Emlyn-Jones and William Preddy (Cambridge, MA: Harvard University Press, 2017).

[6]Many naturalists may balk at my harsh description of the reality of human existence in a world where there is no divinity, but I stand by the harshness. If there is nothing but space dust in varying composites and make ups, then there is nothing but space dust!

[7]John Gray, *Seven Types of Atheism* (New York: Picador, 2019), 21-22.

[8]Fyodor Dostoyevsky, *The Brothers Karamazov* (New York: Penguin, 2003), 198.

[9]See, for example, his book *Morality Without God* (Oxford: Oxford University Press, 2009).

[10]See Nagel, *View from Nowhere*, chaps. 8 and 11, and *The Last Word* (Oxford: Oxford University Press, 1997), chap. 6.

[11]Richard Dawkins, *The Selfish Gene*, 40th anniv. ed. (Oxford: Oxford University Press, 2016), 52.

[12]Michael Ruse, "God Is Dead. Long Live Morality," *The Guardian*, March 15, 2010.

[13]St. Augustine, *City of God* (London: Penguin, 1984), 308.

[14]David Hume, "Of the Standard of Taste" (1757).

[15]Some rightfully ask, "If you don't believe beauty tilts the scales, why dedicate a section of your book to it?" Two reasons: (1) Beauty is often cited by some as an objective reality and a good reason to believe in God. See, e.g., David Skeel, *True Paradox: How Christianity Makes Sense of Our Complex World* (Downers Grove, IL: InterVarsity Press, 2014). So that makes the matter worthy of consideration. (2) My failure to be persuaded illuminates the deductive reasoning I rely upon in these matters, as well as my willingness to abandon that which doesn't align with my reasoning.

[16]See interview, "Outspoken Atheist Asked What He'd Say to God After Death," *The Blaze*, February 1, 2015, www.theblaze.com/stories/2015/02/01/outspoken-atheist -asked-what-hed-say-to-god-after-death-discovering-its-all-true-his-answer -throws-the-interviewer-for-a-loop/.

[17]Fry also serves as a brilliant illustration of my prior evidence about objective right and wrong. Note he speaks of "utter, utter evil." He calls his perception of God's terms as "wrong." These value terms have real objective meaning to Fry. Yet if people are merely sacks of chemicals, Fry's language and concerns are illusory. In modern legal parlance, "There is no there there."

[18]"Post hoc analysis" is a classic logical fallacy always viewed suspiciously. The Latin *post hoc* means "after this." The analysis references forming a view *after* an argument or event often to justify a sought-out conclusion.

[19]For more on this from a legal history perspective, see W. Mark Lanier, *Justice for All*, 52 Tex. Tech L. Rev. (2019).

[20]Here I use *karma* to reference justice in results, not the Eastern concept of reincarnation based upon one's performance in a prior existence. I will examine the Eastern concept in the upcoming volume, *Religions on Trial* (Downers Grove, IL: InterVarsity Press, 2022).

7. HUMAN DIGNITY AND SIGNIFICANCE

[1]Chomsky, Noam, "The Case Against B. F. Skinner," *New York Review of Books*, December 30, 1971.

[2]This is based on the chimpanzees studied at Gombe National Park in Tanzania, the site of Dr. Jane Goodall's groundbreaking work dispelling the myth that chimpanzees were vegetarians. See C.B. Stanford, *Chimpanzee and Red Colobus: The Ecology of Predator and Prey* (Cambridge, MA: Harvard University Press 1998).

[3]Thomas Nagel, *The View from Nowhere* (Oxford: Oxford University Press, 1986), 209.

[4]Albert Camus, *Le Mythe de Sisyphe* (Paris: Gallimard, 1942).

[5]Nagel, *View From Nowhere*, 210.

[6]Nagel, *View From Nowhere*, 209.

[7]Nagel, *View From Nowhere*, 221.

[8]Augustine, *Confessions*, trans. Henry Chadwick (Oxford: Oxford University Press, 1991), 1.1.

[9]Blaise Pascal, *Pensées*, trans. W. F. Trotter (London: Dutton, 1948), 425.

[10]See, "What Does It Mean to Be a Human?," at www.humanorigins.si.edu/education/introduction-human-evolution.

[11]A word of warning about natural selection. I am not suggesting that natural selection is not a reality. Judeo-Christian Scriptures teach that animals were made to propagate after their kind. They are self-sustaining in that regard just as people are. In the earliest story of Adam and Eve, one sees natural selection taking place in the sense that Adam chose the most fit mate for him, not finding one suitable among the animal world until Eve came along. Here, and in other places where I am weighing evidence, my analysis is based on a natural selection that is devoid of any God.

8. THE PROBLEM OF SUFFERING

[1]Bart Ehrman, *God's Problem* (San Francisco: Harper One 2009), 1.

[2]Ehrman, *God's Problem*, 21-22.

[3]Personal correspondence from Dr. Michael Lloyd, principal of Wycliffe Hall, Oxford, December 22, 2020.

[4]Some Bible translations refer to Israel's miraculous exit from Egypt through the "Red Sea," but the Hebrew should more likely be rendered "the Sea of Reeds."

[5]*PDK Laboratories, Inc. v. U.S. Drug Enforcement Administration*, 362 F.3d 786, 799 (D.C. Ct. App. 2004).

[6]Edwin G. Dolan, *TANSTAAFL (There Ain't No Such Thing As A Free Lunch)* (London: Searching Finance, 2011), 190.

10. SCIENCE AND FAITH

[1]Alex Rosenberg, *The Atheist's Guide to Reality: Enjoying Life Without Illusions* (New York: Norton, 2012), 7.

[2]Farr A. Curlin et al., "When Patients Choose Faith Over Medicine: Physician Perspectives on Religiously Related Conflict in the Medical Encounter," *Archives of Internal Medicine* 165, no. 1 (2005): 88-91.

[3]"Israel's neighbors" covers a number of different cultures and civilizations. North and east of Israel were Mesopotamia and the cultures of the Sumerians, the Akkadians, the Amorites, the Assyrians, and the Babylonians. The Hittites were principally north as well. These people existed at the dawn of civilization when writing was first taking form. While scholars know of these people, their origins and roots are somewhat a matter of conjecture. To the south of Israel, the Egyptians were the principal people. Along the western edge of Israel were the coastal neighbors. This region was a melting pot of people bridging the larger national developments of Mesopotamia in the north, Egypt in the south, and even sea-traveling people of the Mediterranean. These people, collectively referred to as people of "Syria-Palestine," included the Philistines, the Arameans, Canaanites, and some Amorite people. A few the city-states in this area have produced ancient texts for study, notably those at Ugarit and Ebla. Scholars speak of these cultures in this time as the "ancient Near East," or "ANE" for short.

[4]Bill T. Arnold, *Encountering the Book of Genesis* (Grand Rapids, MI: Baker Academic, 1998), 49.

[5]S. R. Hirsch, *Commentary on the Torah*, trans. Isaac Levy (New York: Judaica, 1966), 1:2.

[6]Genesis 1 uses a word for God found throughout the Old Testament: *elohim*. This word is plural in form, even though it is used as a singular noun when used of God. Hirsch believes that the plural form is used because in the "One Unique God" are found the "whole plentitude of power of these supposedly numerous *elohims*." Hirsch, *Commentary*, 1:4.

[7]An easy-to-read translation of *The Book of Nut* by James P. Allen is found in William Hallo, ed., *The Context of Scripture: Canonical Compositions from the Biblical World* (Leiden: Brill, 1996), 1:5. Other Egyptian records teach that Shu (the atmosphere) was sneezed out by Atum Scarab. See the pyramid text spells

(1.4) in Hallo, *Context of Scripture*, 1:7. Coffin texts teach the origins of Nut, Shu, and Geb. (Hallo, *Context of Scripture*, 1:10).

[8]"Epic of Creation (Enuma Elish)," in Hallo, *Context of Scripture*, 1:391.

[9]"Epic of Creation (Enuma Elish)," in Hallo, *Context of Scripture*, 1:391.

[10]That isn't to say that God didn't have an ability to control the world and its weather. But God's control over that was the exception, not the rule. Hence the standoff between God and Ba'al described in 1 Kings 18.

[11]"Elkunirsa and Asertu," in Hallo, *Context of Scripture*, 149.

[12]Hallo, *Context of Scripture*, 391.

[13]Hallo, *Context of Scripture*, 400.

[14]"Atra-Hasis," in Hallo, *Context of Scripture*, 450-51.

[15]"The Wrath of Telipinu," in Hallo, *Context of Scripture*, 151.

[16]Ernst Jenni and Claus Westermann, *Theological Lexicon of the Old Testament* (Peabody, MA: Hendrickson, 1997), 3:1297.

[17]"Atrahasis," 208; "Enuma Elish," 6.30.

[18]John H. Walton, *Ancient Near Eastern Thought and the Old Testament: Introducing the Conceptual World of the Hebrew Bible* (Grand Rapids, MI: Baker Academic, 2006), 166. Luis Stadlemann did groundbreaking work on similar analysis in *The Hebrew Conception of the World* (Rome: Biblical Institute Press, 1970). I have charted through much of the analysis of both in this text.

[19]Some myths in Egypt had the sun "swallowed" by the sky goddess Nut each night, moving unseen through her body to be born again each morning.

[20]Izak Cornelius, "The Visual Representation of the World in the Ancient Near East and the Hebrew Bible," *Journal of Northwest Semitic Languages* 20, no. 2 (1994).

[21]See the analysis in Walton, *Ancient Near Eastern Thought*, 205.

[22]Walton, *Ancient Near Eastern Thought*, 212.

[23]The Greek is even a bit more precise in its meaning than is easily conveyed in a word-by-word English translation. The "invisible attributes" that have been "clearly perceived" have a Greek verb in the middle voice. This is not an English voicing of verbs, so it is a challenge for translating into English. In the middle voice, the noun related to the verb is participating to some degree in the action of the verb. The impact of it in a passage like Romans 1:19-20 is that the things that are made are participating in proclaiming the invisible attributes of God. It is written in a way that draws an emphasis to the actual testimony of the creation to the creator.

[24]I am not suggesting that the Bible doesn't allow that God can intervene in the cause-and-effect world. The virgin birth of Jesus is an example of God's intervention. Even then, though, the intervention (i.e., the miraculous pregnancy)

becomes a *part* of the normative cause-and-effect world. Jesus is born, fed, reared, works, gets tired, gets hungry, etc.

11. EVOLUTION

[1]Augustine, *The Literal Meaning of Genesis*, 2 vols., trans. John Hammond Taylor (Mahwah, NJ: Paulist Press 1982), 1:2.

[2]Augustine, *The Literal Meaning of Genesis*, 1:2.

[3]Augustine, *The Literal Meaning of Genesis*, 1:3.

[4]Augustine, *The Literal Meaning of Genesis*, 1:30.

[5]For example, some believe plants in this world were growing by the light of God, citing Revelation 21:23 ("And the city [New Jerusalem] has no need of sun or moon to shine on it, for the glory of God gives it light, and its lamp is the Lamb"). Others counter that this created world is discussed in Genesis 1, and the passage does not speak of God as light in that way in this world. Furthermore, to some it seems pagan to place God into creation as a part of the physical realm rather than a Creator of the physical realm.

[6]Augustine, *The Literal Meaning of Genesis*, 1:41.

[7]Robert Alter, *Genesis: Translation and Commentary* (New York: Norton, 1996), 3.

[8]John C. Collins, *Genesis 1-4: A Linguistic, Literary, and Theological Commentary* (Phillipsburg, NJ: P&R, 2006), 50.

[9]Collins, *Genesis 1-4*, 71-72. Collins also speaks of the "poetic parallelism" and "poetic diction" of Gen 1:1–2:3.

[10]Collins, *Genesis 1-4*, 36, 40-41; Victor P. Hamilton, *The Book of Genesis: Chapters 1-17*, New International Commentary on the Old Testament (Grand Rapids, MI: Eerdmans, 1990), 2-11.

[11]See, e.g., Hamilton, *Book of Genesis*, 53.

[12]Collins, *Genesis 1-4*, 44.

[13]See, e.g., Collins, *Genesis 1-4*, 73.

[14]Collins, *Genesis 1-4*, back cover endorsement.

[15]Hamilton, *Book of Genesis*, 54. The basic and most frequent usage of the Hebrew *yom* ("day") is referring to the time of daylight between sunrise and sunset (for example, Gen 8:22). A lesser usage, but one that is still quite common, is a full twenty-four-hour day (for example, in Num 7:12-78). Further, "in many cases *yom* loses the specific meaning 'day' and becomes a rather general and vague word for 'time, moment.'" Ernst Jenni and Claus Westermann, eds, *Theological Lexicon of the Old Testament* (Peabody, MA: Hendrickson, 1997), 2:527-29.

[16]"Evening and morning bracket the night (see Num 9:15 where 'the appearance of fire' was over the tabernacle *from evening until morning*; in verse 16, we find this paraphrased as 'the appearance of fire [covered the tabernacle] *by night*.' Hence,

night is the period from evening to morning), and this is the daily time of rest for the worker. In Psalm 104:23, when the sun rises, 'man goes out to his work, and to his labor until the evening.'" Collins, *Genesis 1-4*, 77.

[17]In the first centuries of the Christian church, the schools of Alexandria are notable for teaching allegorical interpretations of Scripture as the fullest and most pious way to understand the Bible. Teachers at the Catechetical School of Alexandria like Clement of Alexandria (c. 150–c. 215) and Origen (c. 185–c. 254) emphasized that the greater truths of Scripture were revealed through allegory.

[18]A sometimes-surprising example of allegorical reading is the Christmas carol *We Three Kings*. The song is built, in part, on an allegorical reading of Genesis. The allegorical idea of Abraham's son Isaac representing Jesus allowed the reading of Genesis 26:26 to be the visit by three king/commander types, to be seen as an allegorical precursor to the unquantified magi who visit Jesus in Matthew 2.

[19]Collins, *Genesis 1-4*, 78-79.

[20]Peter Enns, *Inspiration and Incarnation: Evangelicals and the Problem of the Old Testament* (Grand Rapids, MI: Baker Academic 2005), 16.

[21]Enns, *Inspiration and Incarnation*, 18.

[22]Enns, *Inspiration and Incarnation*, 53.

[23]Enns, *Inspiration and Incarnation*, 55.

[24]John H. Walton, *Ancient Near Eastern Thought and the Old Testament: Introducing the Conceptual World of the Hebrew Bible* (Grand Rapids, MI: Baker Academic, 2006), 19-20.

ABOUT THE AUTHOR

W. MARK LANIER IS A PRACTICING TRIAL ATTORNEY who has spent thirty-seven years in courtrooms across America. His record-setting verdicts have made international headlines, winning landmark victories in pharmaceutical and medical litigation, antitrust litigation, fraud, asbestos, and more. With offices in New York, Houston, and Los Angeles, he tries cases in courtrooms across America. He lectures in the leading law schools and is frequently found on Fox Business News, CNN, and other leading news stations. The movie *Puncture* was based on one of his cases.

Mark has a degree in biblical Hebrew and Greek from Lipscomb University, and in addition to his legal writings, is the author of *Christianity on Trial*, the award-winning *Psalms for Living*, and *Torah for Living*.

Mark founded the Lanier Theological Library, one of the world's leading private theological libraries open to the public. The library features lectures from top scholars each year, including a number referenced in this book as well as Justice Scalia, and other notables in the legal, scientific, and religious arenas. Those lectures are available on the library website: www.LanierTheologicalLibrary.org. Mark can be reached at info@lanierfoundation.org or info@Lanierlawfirm.com.

ALSO BY W. MARK LANIER

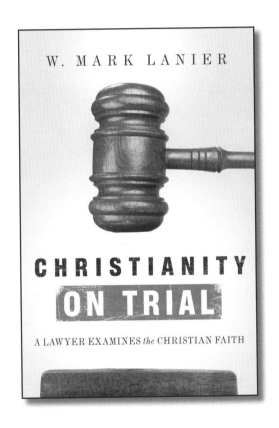